Cash Flow Magic

OR

The Real Secrets of Multiple Streams of Income

Top Biz Guru - Ron G Holland

Author of the international bestsellers:
Talk & Grow Rich and *Turbo Success*

Cover: Perseus Design

Cash Flow Magic

OR

The Real Secrets of Multiple Streams of Income

Ron G Holland

www.wealth.co.uk

Eureka Financial Publishers, Suite 8061, 27 Old Gloucester Street, London WC1N 3XX

Cash Flow Magic

www.wealth.co.uk

CHAPTER ONE

SOME REAL SECRETS OF
MULTIPLE STREAMS OF INCOME

I want to demystify what everyone yearns to know...

How to make extra cash!

I hope through this report you will find many ways of making extra money, ways of increasing your disposable income and start attaining the lifestyle you desire. The report is written in plain language and most importantly is written for the UK market. It is also written from the standpoint of coming from having little or no resources. Over the past few years 'Multiple Streams of Income' has become a real buzzword, and more and more people ask me about it and it appears more and more people find it difficult to accomplish, and instead of getting on the 'bandwagon' find themselves being swept away in a tide of debts and frustration. What I have aimed to do here is provide real tips, clues and guidelines for those wishing to improve their financial status. I also aim to provide enthusiasm, motivation and planning. To do that I want to go back over fifty years to when I was a young lad – and coining it in!

As a schoolboy

As a child I stumbled on the power of multiple streams of income and in a very unsophisticated way developed an income way beyond any of my school chums. I didn't realise it at the time but these early days provide some real useable clues to creating 'Multiple Streams of Income'.

From the age of eleven I would busy myself seven days a week with a paper round. Two rounds on Sundays if I could get them. My forte was being able to ride my bicycle, park it at each house, run in and scoot off again in record time...and this is the important bit, and if it wasn't important I wouldn't mention it, I would whistle from the start of the round until I posted the last newspaper through its respective letter box...I was not only happy in my work, I was ecstatically happy! At Christmas time I used to knock on the customers' doors and ask for a Christmas Box. Most gave generously and many mentioned how they used to love to hear me sing and whistle in the early morning, it lifted their spirit. I used to earn so much money in that one week prior to Christmas my old dad had to help me count it!

On Saturday and Sunday morning and all through the school holidays I used to do a milk round. I was always very cheerful and whistling, which the milkman and the customers often commented on. Again this happy go lucky state of mind is extremely important to mention...you'll see where I am going with this in a minute. Again, at Christmas time, the tips used to flood in...and again, more money than I could count on my own and certainly more money than I knew what to do with!

I was on a roll and everything I touched turned to gold – effortlessly. Every Tuesday after school I would clean the silver for Mrs Sowden – the highlight was that her two daughters, both a little older than me where ever present. Again I'd go home clutching a few coins – having thoroughly enjoyed myself for an hour or two.

At weekends, after my milk round I trawled the council dump where all the school trash was tipped and found literally hundreds of marbles – all of which I washed down, packed up and sold to school chums. I'd sell guinea-pigs, hamsters, kittens and stick insects. All a hoot because I used to love the pets – but the money flowed with each offspring. In my spare time I'd cut logs both for home and for sale and spent time of repairing cycles for school chums.

Empty lemonade and beer bottles had a cash premium on them, if you returned them to the retailer he happily gave you a few coins for each bottle, and they used to gravitate toward me on daily basis...I couldn't keep them away. Another stream of revenue and it just kept coming. I still had plenty of time to collect scrap metal, carry out cycle repairs, and sell second-hand comics, Meccano, bicycle spares and eventually mopeds.

So just what are the lessons of the early days?

Everything was fun; I laughed, sang and whistled... literally all the way to the bank. I was in the zone, life just flowed and I went with the flow. Nothing was hard work, there was no resentment of the work I was carrying out, everything came naturally and every pursuit was like a hobby – and money flooded in. Being carefree and easy going *allowed* money to flow into my life – effortlessly. All the activities complemented one another, there was plenty of time for everything and all the resources I used were a stone's throw from my own home. I blended into the environment and made use of everything that was there.

The next big lesson, and I did this intuitively, was to create massive cash flow with labour intensive activities – then parlay that cash flow into products that could be sold for substantial profits. Products that can make you big profits often require capital to be purchased. Many times that capital, i.e. your grubstake, can come from the labour intensive work. Differentiate between labour intensive work and other activities and work out a plan for working smart - not hard. Obviously if you're supplying labour in exchange for money you'll be severely limited to the amount you can earn, after all there are so many hours in a day. Start thinking how to parlay hard earned cash into profitable products.

The third big lesson, and you'll notice this pattern repeat itself over and over again, is that when you are in the zone, going with the *flow,* all the streams of income link effortlessly together and eventually all lead into one big river that leads to the sea. This is how nature works and it is important to recognize because the last thing you want to do is spread yourself too thin and be scurrying around like a headless chicken doing loads of unrelated activities. The ideal is to have many of cash generating business that all enhance each other.

As an apprentice

I left school at the age of fourteen and signed up as an apprentice carpenter and joiner. They wages were very low to begin, quite literally a couple of pounds a week. Very quickly I got into motorcycles and started racing. This was an expensive pastime and I soon had to subsidise my apprentice wages. Quickly, I set up an odd jobs business doing all sorts of carpentry jobs in my spare time with my new found skills. I also started a scrap metal business and found that once I got into it I found scrap everywhere...without even trying. I even found some old lead on the church roof! This was nice little earner and because of my unlimited budget, soon my motorcycle racing flourished. As my passion developed, I found myself repairing other people's motorcycles and also buying motorcycles to resell...at a huge profit would you believe?

As an entrepreneur

The day I finished my carpentry apprenticeship I opened my first motorcycle shop in West Ewell, Surrey, and, as they say, the rest is history. Very quickly I ended up with seven motorcycle shops and a couple of pick-up-trucks. I hated to see the trucks under-utilised so I set up two second-hand furniture shops in Wimbledon and Wandsworth and the trucks were employed on house clearing duty. This was great fun, hugely profitable – and yet another stream of income. As a result of over spending on my racing motorcycles, the shops got into financial difficulty. Fortuitously for me, I bumped into an astute old Irishman, Seamus O'Rourke, who helped me turn the company around. At the end of the very successful turnaround I wrote a book, Debt Free with Financial Kung Fu, about the experience which I sold through mail order...another stream of income and one that is still bringing in a stream of royalties and consultancy work after thirty years! I couldn't stop it even if I tried!

On the back of the book Seamus and I set up a business consultancy and we soon found we could not only earn good fees but in many instances gets ourselves 50% of various companies for coming in on a partnership basis, not just as consultant. We had more streams of revenue than you could poke a stick at.

As a consultant and financial author

I advise people to do whatever it takes...many times getting the first steam of revenue flooding in by doing something labour intensive. Fine, if you have some capital and can immediately invest in products to resell for a handsome profit - but most people haven't got access to capital. You have to start with the tools and resources that are available to you, simple as that. I really do consider myself privileged in so far as I have had the opportunity to talk to thousands of people of a thirty-year period. Many just cannot get their minds around that the role models they look up to often started with nothing and had to create their first stream of income through hard physical work. I have also talked to the rich and famous and they are in awe that they see so many people wishing, hoping, praying – but not jumping into action and they express to me that these people could get everything they wanted out of life...if only they would start work.

Who's the man who sells the salt?

I love the story concerning the consultant who went into a flagging retail store and quizzed the owner about all the stocks of salt on the shelves. In essence he said, 'Wow, you must sell a lot of a salt. You've got three shelves full of the stuff here...and two on the other side of the store. You have salt piled up by the door and there are four cases of salt in the back storeroom. Wow you must sell a lot of salt...in actual fact you must be the best salt salesman in the country.' The embarrassed store owner replied, 'No, in actual fact I hardly ever sell any salt at all. The guy who really sells a lot of salt is the guy who sells me the salt. Now there's a guy who really sells a lot of salt!'

Stop buying main dealer packs - start selling them!

This story follows on from the previous and it concerns all the proprietary 'Get Rich Quick' packages that are available today. Buy this one and become a 'Property Tycoon.' Buy another that leads you onto being a 'Master Practitioner' or another leads you on to becoming a 'Master Success Coach'. These main dealer packages make one person rich and that is for sure that's the person who was bright and entrepreneurial enough to start the scheme. Don't forget I'm all for it - as long I can convince you of one thing. If you are going to be rich and create Multiple Streams of Income the sooner you can start your own scheme (whatever it is!) and start taking money off other people the sooner you will be on your way! This programme is only about one thing – helping you to do just that - and remember where you heard it first!

Every time I hear a Master Practitioner or Business Success Coach introduce himself to me I can't help saying, 'Wow, that's fantastic, now you're on the first rung of the ladder you've really got your work cut out!

What you have to do now is actually start using those skills and actually putting them into practice in the real world. For instance what I suggest is that you *really* start visualising, in great detail and see yourself in the picture of you actually selling main dealer packs of your own. The same as the guy who originally created the brilliant pack that he sold to you for £5k or £10k or, if you were one of the chosen few, the £15k package. You really need to get into visualisation and use it properly, if you are going to pay of the credit card bill that allowed you to buy the package in the first place. Next you need to hone up on those Auditory skills – because as you'll very quickly come to realise, out in the real world it's not all about telling glossy stories and metaphors, but telling a story the punters will really buy into, part with *their* £5k, £10k or £15k and be so pleased with your product they won't want their money back.'

The biggest lesson to be learned on the purchase of a main dealer package, of course, is modelling, and I suggest you model the guy who sold you the pack in the first place. He's got a revenue stream formula that's working and it doesn't take rocket science to work out a 100 main dealer packages at £8k a pop is £800,000 yes...with a little more imagination and hard, work that's nearly a million – now you know the real formula, maybe you can do better! This is what you need as just one of your revenue streams.

Use your newly earned visualization techniques to 'see' in your imagination, the original promoter (sitting at his kitchen table, in his underwear; this is how great ideas are concocted!) plotting and planning and scheming and scamming on how to put a package together that would start coining it in and creating him multiple streams of income. 'See' him making mock up packages out of cardboard, writing killer app copy, googling copywriters and making up dummy sales letters...all this went on believe me before he came up with his successful main dealer pack and believe me this process is what you will have to go through if you are to create multiple streams of income. Envelopes containing cash and credit card orders don't just come flooding through your letterbox unless you go through the process – and I have just described the process to you!

At first light this is a huge revelation and is, perhaps, a bitter pill to swallow, but after all that's what you're paying me for, and I am proud to bring you pragmatic tools – if it brings success, happiness and multiple streams of income into your life.

Aptitude

Do what you love and have a passion for; this is crucial. I have never seen anyone create multiple streams of income and real wealth doing something they hated. Do something you can do. Now that sounds simple enough but you'd be amazed at the number of people who come up to me at the end of my seminars and tell me they have been sold a property development course or an internet marketing course or some other proposition they have no interest in, no skills at, nor any aptitude for. You'll never be able to whistle and sing all day long doing something you loathe and find difficult and see no rewards for and don't forget that it's being in that happy carefree space that allows the money to FLOW.

Mix & match

I love going into businesses and studying them and trying to get into the minds of the owners – especially where they have developed multiple streams of income. I notice more and more bookstores these days selling coffee and cake, very expensive cake, I hasten to add; certainly more profit margin is attainable than in the core product, books. I was at fuel merchants the other day, where they sell coal and fuel oils and other fuels as well. Their secondary business was that of a travel agent and I thought how wonderfully these two businesses complimented one another. One set of staff, one lot of overheads, one premises – two streams of revenue. My local optician has opened up a dentistry practice in the same store...marvellous – I predict this will catch on all over the country – mark my words! How many times have you been into the cobblers to get shoes repaired – now he's a locksmith as well. He understands the value of multiple streams of income, the power of diversification. I see more and more pubs selling food as their main product and Internet Cafes selling coffee and Danish and setting up as money transfer agents. Everywhere I go I notice diversification and multiple streams of income – it is an obsession and a passion and I am always on the lookout for more strings to add to my own bow – as long I can sense cash flow, profit - and fun!

Capacity for hard work

I have noted that successful entrepreneurs, actors, businessmen, netpreneurs all have a massive capacity for hard work. The days run into evenings and the evenings run into night. The weekdays run into weekends and there seems no division. There's no saying 'Wow, it's 5 o'clock! Time to down tools!' Everything is seamless, like being involved in one fantastic holiday or hobby that is so much fun you just don't want it to end. You get into this mode and start thinking of all the things you love to do and wish you could do and start googling those things and visualising those things and seeing yourself being part of those things and suddenly you too will come up with all sorts of particular ideas for streams on income that had been evading you previously. Streams of income start with a stream of consciousness.

I just haven't got the enthusiasm

Over the years I have met many entrepreneurs who yearn for multiple streams of income and when I talk to them about all the things I do and love doing and then I relay what various clients, associates and friends of mine do, many times they look at me wearily and say, I just haven't got the enthusiasm. I want to share a big secret with you and it's this. The secret of enthusiasm is to act enthusiastically whether you are or not. That's the crucial key. Pretend you are enthusiastic! Force yourself to be enthusiastic! Act enthusiastic! Once you do this something incredible will start to happen, genuine enthusiasm will begin to grin through and that's when the real power kicks in.

Understand the different types of revenue streams

Try to get to grips with the opportunities you face because there are thousands of them and they are all different and all have different implications.

Labour intensive revenues streams

This is usually the starting point for individuals trying to create multiple stream of income – especially when they have limited resources. It doesn't take too much imagination to be able to come up with something to do and earn money from. I could write a book on this one subject alone but let me give you a starter for ten.

Can you offer to do gardening, carpentry jobs, odd jobs, window cleaning, looking after the sick, car cleaning, car repairs, sewing, hairdressing, lawn mowing, house cleaning, hedge trimming, ceramic tiling or photography?

Labour intensive – other people supplying labour

I have a client by the name of John who runs a labour intensive business but doesn't do any of the manual graft himself. He supplies office cleaners to some of the largest companies in the North East and he turns over millions of pounds. John has multiple income streams but he swears his cleaning business is the most lucrative and equally the simplest to manage. John himself makes himself busy for a few hours a week bringing on board new customers and signing up the cleaning contract. He finds his customer pay on the nail and this business is so cash generative it allows him to dabble and experiment with other exciting opportunities.

Royalty income

Most people immediately think of writing a book to generate royalties, and the obvious targets are Business Opportunities, Finance and How to Get Rich. Don't ignore Health and Diet, Love, Romance and Sex. Marketing, Advertising and Selling are also huge revenues pullers and so are Fitness, Music, Sport and Religion. I still pull in royalties on a monthly basis from books that I wrote over thirty years ago. And the royalties are the small part of the revenue stream that the right types of books create. I get far more from profile, credibility, prestige, consultancy and deals than I do from the actual royalties...but more about that later.

I know people who have earned small (and large) fortunes writing songs, computer software and games. Others I know have royalty income coming in from products that they have made or had manufactured and sold to the big chains, like B&Q, Home Base, Mother Care or Argos. Bear in mind if you create something and sell it on license to a chain, you may only get 3% - 5% royalty, but it's another revenue stream and if you can keep coming up with ideas for products you'll laugh all the way to the bank. If you sign a deal with a major publisher you can expect 5% to 15%. I have over twenty deals with various publishers with various deals in between the 5% to 15%. If you publish yourself expect 50% to 90% of the revenues after manufacturing costs so you can see why most of my efforts these days are devoted to publishing and promoting my own products!

Rental income

Most people think in terms of property rental, but I know people who make money renting out single rooms, lock up garages, retail shops and commercial premises. I know of others who rent executive jets, light aircraft, speedboats and super yachts. In most instances they don't own these expensive toys themselves but they rent them out on behalf of their owners. Like a broking service and make huge commissions in doing so...with no risk or capital outlay other than having to create customers cost effectively. Others rent pictures from a picture library, others rent videos, machine tools, plant, equipment, champagne glasses for parties and events, lawn mowers, cars, vans, motorcycles, roller blades – in actual fact just about everything you could ever think of. And perhaps that last sentence is a major clue. You may not have bent your mind to what you can rent out, create a streams of income from and have a lot of fun...and perhaps the time has come to do just that.

Retail income

I know so many entrepreneurs who started out in retail, and it isn't funny. Retail is an ideal proving ground for young and old alike. All you need to do is cobble together few months' rent and you're up and running....Yes! Really! Don't make this hard work! With so many suppliers out there it is relatively easy to get stock flooding into your premises on credit and if you find it difficult, my advice is to spread your net further until you find a distributor who'll play ball.

My favourite story was in my early days in the mid-seventies when I had seven motorcycle showrooms and ran out of money. My tunnel vision kept me thinking that I needed to raise capital so I could fill my empty shops and I tried every bank, venture capital house, suppliers of stocking finance and financial institution in the City. I never raised a bean. I was desperate so intuitively I started to visualise my showrooms full of motorcycles. Hey Presto! I had a Eureka! My small still voice said, 'Go out and buy all the motorcycle papers and phone every classified advertisement. Ask the guys if they still have their bikes for sale. If they do, get them to bring their bikes in, say you have salesmen, showroom facilities, insurance and financing facilities and very quickly you'll sell their bikes for them and you'll take a commission.' Hundreds of motorcycles flooded into my showrooms and the rest of the story is the rest of the story...I became a legend in my own lunchtime! Ask yourself the question what stock could you attract to yourself on a Sale or Return Basis? Do you know what – you're only limited by your own imagination!

Absentee ownership business revenue streams

I love absentee ownership businesses and the ones that spring to mind are Laundromats, ice cream vans, Internet cafes, Vending Machines, Games arcades, swimming pools, snooker halls and mini-cab companies. A good exercise is to trawl the local towns in your area and poke you head in a load of doors of business establishments and ask to see the boss. Many times you'll get 'He only comes in at five o'clock' or 'He only comes in on Thursday's' and you'll start to see what I mean. Many businesses can and do run themselves and the owner just goes in to pick up the cash. Is this a revenue stream that may work for you?

Arts and crafts income

Did you know there are hundreds of people in the UK who paint, weave, draw and manufacture all sort of art and craft products and sell them at car boot sales, in the local shops, country stores, farms, nurseries gardens, art fairs and on the Internet? Are you creative? Are you good with your hands? Can you turn your hand to creating something that others would love to own? Have you got skills that you can turn to cash?

Subscription income

I love subscription income and have had it as part of my armoury for many years. My favourite is newsletters, but you may prefer e-zines, membership clubs, magazine subscriptions, wine club subscription for twelve bottles of wine a month. Can you set up a gun club, dating agency or private members club?

Teaching revenues

Can you teach people the piano or guitar or some other musical instrument? Could you teach people some specific computer programme, maths or elocution? Do you have skills that would enable you to teach ballet, dancing, and singing or to act? Can you teach people how to juggle or be a clown or how to meditate or mediate or drive? I can think of numerous people in all these categories who are raking it in – hand over fist. Could you do the same or perhaps a variation on the theme? People do pay to be taught skills and often they pay handsomely!

Success Coaching and Mentoring Revenue Streams

Success Coaching is big business these days and providing you have good listening skills and are good with people and understand how to motivate and inspire you will go a long way. My advice is to write a book on the subject, put out a regular e-zine and blog, create some results for someone, and build a profile.

Consultancy revenue streams

Over the years I have helped literally dozens of people create good income streams in the arena of consultancy, which is a £12bn, a year business in the UK and is booming. I often work with people who have been made redundant and many of these people have years of industry experience and are sitting on a little gold mine. They often don't realize the years of experience the have gained can be packaged in a very lucrative manner and taken to their own particular niche market. My own niche consultancy business lends itself to many streams of revenue and I'll give you just a few examples. I specialise in raising funds for early stage and start-up companies. My first income stream is that I insist on a mobilisation fee when I start the assignment, this is usually £10k to £60k but the size usually depends on how many millions I have been asked to raise. I also get a success fee when I have raised the money and this may range anything from 3% to 8% and this is paid at the completion of the funding. I also negotiate some shares and options in every company that I raise money for. I may get various other commissions along the way as I introduce bank finance, factoring, PR, marketing experts, advertising agencies and other professional advisers. I usually receive say between 5% and 15% of their billing...depending on what I can negotiate!

Salesman's revenue streams

Selling is one of those great things that can allow you to earn huge incomes especially if you are either good at it or very tenacious. Top flight salesmen earn huge amounts selling cars, houses, commercial property, land, advertising space, foreign exchange, shares, currency, property, aeroplanes, yachts, timeshare, vacations, insurance, health products, and office equipment. The list is endless but the point is what could you get enthusiastic about and passionate about enough to be able to explain to people the benefits of the product or service in such a way they would sign a contract or buy the product from you. The great thing about selling is that you are using your valuable time to create much more money that if you were using on some manual task...there really isn't a comparison to the amount of money that can be earned in this way.

The amazing thing about selling is that there are huge numbers of opportunities that abound and most of them will willingly take on new comers to the game especially if you are game, personable and willing to learn and put the hours of confrontation time in. The key is being a good listener and mimic what other good salesmen are already doing in the field you are endeavouring to break into. If you have any nous at all you will be able to pick up, mirror and act.

eBay and eBay with difference

Well over 40,000 people have quit their jobs to sell products and earn a living with E-bay and I think that's just brilliant. There are now over 50,000 people selling products on eBay in the UK alone. Also what I like about eBay is that it is a business you can start with no capital and that's a big plus. The first time I heard about any kind of success to do with eBay was on a Christmas trip to Lapland with my family and on the coach from the airport to the log cabins I heard two women excitedly swapping stories about how one, on her first sale, bought a box of tin soldiers for £100 and sold them the same week on eBay for £1200. That grabbed my attention! The other woman was doing even better, not as much profit margin, but shifting huge volumes of designer clothing. Now, make no mistake about it, these women were computer literate and knew exactly what they were doing. On my return I mentioned these stories to my mate Bob and his son has just sold a diamond on E-Bay for £750 making about £250 profit – beginners luck? - It's too early to say! The latest story I heard was a guy offering to sell your products on eBay for you, for a commission - and the stories go on and on.

My advice is that if you are computer literate and are excited about the Internet, check this one out because it's an idea that really does have legs and could create huge cash flow for you. Be professional, study shipping rates, methods and prices and keep those shipping cost reasonable. Offer many methods of payment including all credit card facilities. Use a high quality picture to promote the product you are selling but equally as important write the best copy that you can. Building up good feedback is crucial to successful selling on eBay so do everything you can to give five star customer service.

Apparently there are some really good publications in the market place about how to trade on eBay and I am a great believer in self education....but my best advice would be begin trading on eBay and start to read and study at the same time...but start trading...that's the key in all of this – MAKE A START!

Talk & grow rich

Has it ever occurred to you that when you listen to an after dinner speaker or a seminar leader or listen to a teleconference call someone somewhere is earning money...yes another revenue stream can be gained from speaking engagements and I've been talking and growing rich for over twenty five years and yes I wrote a book about it! If you have a story to tell, have the gift of the gab, love talking in front of people, you should bend your mind as to where income can come from this amazing talent you have. These day many big cruise ships pay handsomely to those who can come and talk for an hour or two on a variety of subjects and there are many business lunches now that employ top flight professionals such as racing drivers, actors, T.V. personalities, sportsmen to come and entertain for an hour or an hour and a half. Create your own story and own niche and think where you may fit in.

Don't say 'I can't do that' because at the end of the day you're going to have to do something! Nature advertises in the trees, plants, animals and human beings. You must evolve or become extinct. Do something, change, alter, evolve but get to grips with your environment or DIE. If necessary re-invent yourself like Madonna does practically every other week and keep re-inventing yourself and adapting to your environs and circumstances until you do get where you want to go. Survival of the fittest!

Mail order revenues

When you get into discussion with most people their minds are usually drawn toward books and business information products, but the story and the potential is much bigger than that, in actual fact mail order books are just the tip of a multi-billion-pound iceberg. I accidentally discovered mail order years back when I had my seven motorcycle shops. Every week we'd run an advert in the motorcycle press for all the spares we had for sale. As we'd break a bike up we'd list the wheels and engines and forks and generators and gearboxes and put a price on them and put them in Motorcycle News thinking that maybe bikers would come in and buy them. They did in droves – but even bigger droves of enthusiasts put the money in the post and asked us to ship the parts all over the UK. I can tell you that the hardest thing to wrap in corrugated cardboard is a rear wheel from a Norton Commando or pair of front forks off a 750cc Honda, but we managed OK and shipped the stuff via British Rail and the Post Office...this was long before the likes of DHL, UPS and TNT. When we shipped complete engines we learned the secret of draining off all the oil first...that saved us no end of problems and trouble...but we had to learn first! This mail order revenue stream was an unexpected bonus to my retail revenues, but once I recognised it I wanted to capitalise on it.

Fortuitously for me I purchased a copy of Joe Karbo's *Lazy Man Way to Riches* not even knowing it was about the mail order business. It was another turning point in my life because not only did I get to grips with selling second-hand motorcycle spares through the post in a much more professional way I also wrote, as Joe suggested, a little book about something I was passionate about. I had just turned my flagging shops around with the help of Seamus and I was passionate about business and getting out of debt. I wrote **GET OUT OF DEBT AND INTO THE MONEY** and it sold like hot cakes using full page adverts in *Exchange and Mart* with the headline Cash Flow Problems - Creditors Putting on Pressure. Thirty years on, with the new title of *Debt Free with Financial Kung Fu* it's still pulling in royalties from all over the world in book, e-book, CD, PDF and MP3 audio download formats. The book went so well I then created a catalogue solely for the purpose of selling sex toys and that little venture went quite well although I never really capitalised on its potential. My mind was then focused on going to the States and writing *Talk and Grow Rich* and becoming a full time writer, which leads me onto the next part of Mail Order revenue streams.

Soon after settling in America, having arrived in Beverly Hills, Los Angeles on the West coast, after three months I found myself on the East coast in Boston Massachusetts where I promptly set up mail order catalogue called the APPRENTICE MILLIONAIRES CLUB. It was a full 60 pages and filled with hundreds of books and manuals about making money, self-help, health, positive thinking – all the good stuff and I sent out the first 10,000 catalogues. I can't remember the exact figures but quite a lot of money and orders rolled in, but when I added it all up I just could not for the life of me see that it was going to be a profitable enough venture for me. I toyed with the idea of rolling out 50,000 or 100,000 catalogues but in the end I decided to cut my losses and call it a day. The truth is it didn't make a loss, it even made small a PROFIT, but I couldn't see the wood for the trees. Silly me! I walked away from a mail order FORTUNE because knowing what I know today, I was on an absolute winner. I just couldn't see it at that moment in time. I was hung up on greed for money right now – I didn't realise the mail order business is one where the real money is made from your own list of customers that you milk, year after year, after year – once you have captured their names and addresses and satisfied them.

Create a green machine of your own

I love the term *Green Machine* because to me it always conjures up the image of a Heath Robinson type machine with flywheels and valves and steam belching out – while at the business end out pops a flood of greenback - £50 notes or $100 bills. *Green Machine, Green Machine, Green Machine,* say this mantra over and over again! It pays to have the image and the words as part of your vocabulary. If I had had this consciousness about me in the early days of setting up THE APPRENTCIE MILLIONAIRES CLUB catalogue I would have taken a step back. Maybe even taken a few days off, strolled on the beach and thought through the consequences of what was happening and what I was doing. I had the makings of a green machine in my hands and maybe you can learn from this valuable lesson. What tweaks can you do to your own business to make it better, quicker more efficient and more profitable? In effect what can you do to turn it into a green machine? Can you franchise it? Can you add products or services or maybe take some away. Can you set up a mail order arm or foreign division? Can you change the model? Can you go from 17% to 117% to 1117% profit? I did with my motorcycle shops – remember?

Neal relishes in it!

Neal, who I have known for a number of years relishes in his streams of income and he's looking for more. His main bag is that for a few hours a week he repairs people's baths...he re-enamels them and brings them up like new. Incidentally, Neal paid to learn this skill as he perceived it would be more lucrative than carpet fitting, his previous line. He does perhaps two to seven a week with really trying and this brings a good cash flow... and he's never looked back. He has a number of income properties that he rents out and when the mortgages are paid there is even a little pocket money left over. Early morning and late evening he spends an hour or two spread betting and is making small profits. Neal is now concentrating on Internet related opportunities and he has some specific computer skills and aptitude relating to this....it comes as a second nature to Neal, so I'm pretty sure he'll do it when he finds the right niche. Neal knows what he is looking for and that is a 'killer app' that he can roll out in a big way...and make his home run £500,000 to £1,000,000.

You can't do this without a mentor

I was the closing speaker at the Entrepreneurs Convention in London Earls Court last year and the speaker before me was multi-millionaire property tycoon Andy Hunt of ClearSky properties. He was talking to the packed auditorium about building a property empire. Andy specialises in selling properties in Florida, Bahamas and Canada. He has a thriving business and in actual fact he has taken revenues from the property business and invested in an earthworm farm as well as some Internet opportunities. All the way through his talk, which was entitled by the way, *You can't do this without a mentor*, Andy put huge emphasis on attracting and getting the right mentor on board. I wondered where he was leading with all this because he kept alluding to having the right mentor and kept saying "I'll tell you more about this at the end." His closing statements were along the lines of "My mentor helped me start from nothing, before we had sold a single property and held my hand until we had our first million in the bank account – in actual fact he's your next speaker, please put your hands together and give Ron G Holland a warm welcome." I couldn't have asked for a better introduction than that and I'm pleased to be part of Andy's success.

My advice to you is to get a mentor on board as soon as is practical. Someone you can trust to give you good advice, hold your hand inspire and motivate you and give you the right kind of feedback at the right time. You need to look around for role models, people in business, and those who already have multiple streams of income. What you need to do next is to befriend them and ask them to be your mentor. Once you have a mentor, don't drive them mad, listen to them, try to follow their advice. Respect your Mentor's time and offer thanks on a regular basis and show appreciation by offering a lunch or coffee or by sending a card.

Do your own thinking!

A lot of any success philosophy is often contradictory. For arguments sake, in the previous paragraphs I have been talking about taking advice and heeding mentors –

powerful stuff. Now I am talking about doing your own thinking – equally as powerful. In my business career that spans over four decades it hasn't passed my attention that most people don't do their own thinking. That's why business opportunity seminars and franchise seminars are always packed to capacity. People looking for a quick fix - 'show me what I've got to do at nine o'clock in the morning to start earning money. Show me a-paint-by-number system or a turn-key operation – where I don't have to do any thinking'. Every now and then some do strike it lucky and you're sure to hear all about it. However, what really comes to my attention are the entrepreneurs who go quietly on their way, studying, thinking and planning and conceiving something that is really unique and suddenly they have multiple streams of revenue - cash to cobble dogs with!

My thinking process is definitely about listening to mentors and other people along the way...gathering all sorts of intelligence along the way. I then find it absolutely essential to assimilate, think about and meditate on for long periods of time – combined with powerful visualisation of what I am really trying to create and make happen in my life. It's essential to combine the wisdom of mentors and other people and doing your own thinking and listening to my own 'small still voice' that enables me to come up with ideas and solutions for my own and other people's business problems.

The internet is only a small part of the story... don't get hung up on it!

I notice a huge number of opportunities about making money on the Internet. Unfortunately, most of these opportunities are feeding off each other and they are all showing people the same thing – how to get rich on the Internet. I'm not too sure how many of the purveyors of these schemes are actually selling products and services on the Internet other than the ones that show people how to make money on the Internet. I personally think the Internet is great and have been involved with it since day one. We were the first company to raise money in the UK for an Internet company but we were three years ahead of our time. I have mentioned before, that if you are computer literate, and love the Internet, then yes, by all means explore and experiment and try to see what you can do to sell services or products – but whatever you do, don't get hung up about the Internet because it is still a very small part of an overall business picture that is massive. By just focusing in on the Internet, you will be missing out on a world of other opportunities that is equally as massive.

CHAPTER TWO

**SEED CORN – WHERE DOES START-UP
FINANCE COME FROM?**

Only recently I had my four-year old daughter Kay, on my knee, and as usual was taking every advantage to turn fun into a learning experience. We were sitting by a magnificent gnarled old British Oak that had thousands, perhaps tens of thousands of acorns on it. We picked one up and I talked Kay through, in great detail, about how everyone of these seedpods had the potential to turn into a stately oak, such as the one we were sitting under. I further embellished the story by explaining, just like the parable in the bible, that many seeds end up on stones, some in thistles, some get shrivelled up and only a few that find a proper home in soil, getting sufficient water and sunshine and are nurtured, actually amount to anything.

Our discussion moved on rapidly, because seed corn was on my mind, about how such a tiny acorn could grow into such a big oak tree. Although only four my little daughter is highly articulate, I must confess she struggled in the conversation about how many times bigger the oak tree was than the acorn. I myself struggled with the figures involved when we started talking about maybe a thousand times increase in growth; could it be tens of thousands times increase in growth or perhaps as much as a million times. Incredible things happen in nature, as many a farmer will verify, when he sows a small amount of seed corn across a freshly ploughed field and has it yield a bumper crop.

Seed corn funding is exactly the same and over a long period of time I have come to understand this import aspect of creating wealth. The aspect of seed corn that most people don't realise is that you only need a little to be able to start a business and get yourself onto a level whereby many other funding factors, such as loans, cash-flow, overdrafts and venture capital can come into play. Seed corn funding is the lifeblood of business and every business must start with it. Seed corn is like priming an old-fashioned water pump. You only need to pour half a bucket of water into the pump to prime it, and then by rapidly pumping the handle you will be able to draw water from the well. Without priming the pump you'll be there all day.

The other aspect of seed corn that most people really haven't taken on board is that the same can happen in business as it does with frequency in nature, that when invested and nurtured intelligently, a tiny amount of seed corn can yield massive financial rewards. It strikes me that some cultures know intuitively they must do whatever it takes to cobble together that initial seed corn and get into business on one's own account or invest in another's for massive growth.

I have been to New York many times and have had the privilege of taking the ferry past the Statue of Liberty to Ellis Island, the reception centre for more than 16 million immigrants during its short history from 1882 to

1954, and doing the tour of the Ellis Island Immigration Museum to see where immigrants, many of them Jewish, flooding into New York were processed. This is where they underwent intrusive medical examinations and many times forced name changes to make their names more understandable and acceptable to the American way.

Having listened intently to my host's hundreds of stories it became apparent that many of these immigrants had a built in programme that was to get an income by all means, often taking whatever work was available, in the first instance to sustain themselves and their families, but absolutely driven to save up a seed corn fund to enable them to start a business on their own account.

Immigrants these days still have built in programmes and no matter where in the world, you can see similar things happen. If you drive down Edgware Road in London, early any weekday, even on freezing frost bitten mornings, you will see gangs of Irish, Polish, Albanians, Romanians, Croatians, Latvians and other workers all waiting to be taken to farms, factories and building sites all over London and indeed the Home Counties. I have taken time out to talk to and to listen to many of them, and the same old story comes out. They have come to where the money is and after a short time they will have saved enough seed corn funding to enable them to set up a business on their own account, whatever that business may be.

To a man, they know about Chutzpah. Waiting on the side of a street in a country that is foreign to them, not being able to speak the language, freezing cold, a family maybe thousands of miles away, just waiting for the 'word'. And the only reason why they are there is seed corn, and that's enough!

You probably won't recognise the faces, because immigrants have an age old tradition of assimilating themselves into society and getting on with business, but the chances are in six or twelve months' time you'll be dining in a swish restaurant, or perhaps drinking in an exotic bar, getting your car repaired in a fully equipped body shop, maybe buying a computer from an office supply store or staying at an hotel in a fashionable part of Brighton that was started with seed corn capital, earned on a building site or factory somewhere in London.

Seed corn attracts ideas, business and investment opportunities

Along with a burning desire to accumulate seed corn will come an acute awareness of what is available in the big wide world of business and investment opportunities. As you work away at collecting your seed corn, you will start attracting those opportunities and you can start investigating them, as well understanding your own aptitude. You will also come to realise that there are as many, if not more, schemes and scams and unscrupulous people ready to rip you off from your seed corn as there are genuine opportunities. More on becoming astute later; however for now, the main agenda is to get seed corn capital behind you. An old Yiddish proverb states; with money in the bank, you are wise, you are handsome, and you sing well, too!

Keep in mind the principle of principal

All the time you are gathering your seed corn fund, just know, absolutely know, that seed corn has the potential to multiply up thousands upon thousands of times no matter how small the amount of money that fund is. Also bear in mind that when you start your seed corn fund gathering, the actual business, or business or investment opportunity may not even be on the radar. Imagine those thousands of immigrants flooding into the USA we talked about earlier. They couldn't have possibly known what fate awaited them. All they knew was they wanted a better life, freedom, a business of their own. They developed an acute sense of awareness looking out for and investigating opportunities.

If you already have a job that is sustaining you and your family don't be too eager to give it up prematurely. The secret is to take on more tasks, create extra revenue streams that allow you to build reserves. Save capital at every opportunity, to allow you to start your own business when you see the opportunity you have been seeking or come up with the idea that you think has potential.

Intent, intent, intent

My best advice is to take on board with absolute Intent that one must make a mission of getting hold of seed corn funding. To build that Intent one must constantly keep the goal in mind. Focus on the business you want to start or even better focus on the rewards you want to business to produce. By building a burning desire you will find creative ways of making and saving money. Most people do the opposite. They programme themselves by running a tape loop that says, 'What's the use, I can't even sustain my family, there are bills to pay, food, clothing and shelter to pay for. Everyday life is a struggle.' Those who succeed intentionally take time out to create a burning desire and often a paradigm shift that will get them onto the track they desire that leads to abundance. I personally have spent hundreds of thousands of hours listening to audio tapes that I narrated myself with specific goals I wanted to achieve, and I can honestly say I have often be astounded with the results.

Have a yard sale or car boot sale

Most would-be-entrepreneurs have garages, lockups, bedrooms and back yards full of bits and bobs that can be sold to raise seed corn. Old bicycles, mirrors, paintings, air guns, cots, prams, toys, Airfix models, fish tanks, skate boards, power tools, records, board games, furniture, books and fishing rods are only instruments to enable you to get the cash flowing. It takes real Chutzpah to sell off a few heirlooms, kids toys, terracotta pots and TV sets and other things you deem to be too precious to let go. But this philosophy is all about making it happen, paying the price and doing the right thing, and creating for yourself, what could be the opportunity of a lifetime. Without seed corn, you'll be the proud owner of a J.O.B. for the rest of your life! (**J**ust **O**ver **B**roke!)

The hole in the wall gang

There have been many successful businesses started with seed corn funding that has been acquired through credit card loans. Many times this can be a very expensive form of money but there is an old saying, 'What price money, when you haven't got any?' If you play your cards right, this may very well be the line of least resistance for you, but before you use money at a high rate of interest, do everything in your power to make sure your business will kick in from the word go, and make high returns to repay the interest.

Push out all the boundaries

I have mentioned immigrants many times and I want you to think for a while, to discover the important message. Often it means operating in a strange, sometimes hostile environment. Many times there are language barriers and maybe even laws that get in the way. Often there is verbal and physical abuse to overcome; many times immigrants take on work far below their station. But Chutzpah kicks in and the words 'burning desire, seed corn and start a business of my own' are the fuel that carries one forward and allows one to blank the mind of temporary discomfort. Because of the language barriers laws are not fully understood or maybe they are just ignored because freedom is in grasp maybe for the first time in the immigrants life and paying that price for freedom is justified, calculated and often worth paying. Maybe you will have to pay a price for your own financial freedom, but only you can decide whether that price is worth paying or not.

Trite but true

It is true that often we are sitting on 'acres of diamonds' in our own back yards. A number of my seminar attendees have shared with me stories of how they created revenues way beyond the seed corn stage by exploiting what was at their feet. Lynn was a dab hand in her kitchen at home and was always congratulated on her tasty food, especially her sandwiches. Lynn decided to create tasty sandwiches and first started a small round serving businesses and factories on a local industrial estate. This soon proved to be very popular and Lynn set up her own pitch with a permanent wagon on it selling 'bacon sarnies' and teas from 8am to 6pm. She made small fortune. Her one big regret? She didn't start it sooner!

Bill was a keen gardener and he saw a wonderful opportunity for 'organic crops'. It didn't take him long to organise his garden and allotment to be fully utilised to produce beautiful organic tomatoes, squash, leeks, asparagus, garlic, potatoes, which he sold to a local store, fresh every day. Mary Anne started making 'mountain men' out of scraps of wood, wool, and cloth and she sold these at local tourist outlets. Stewart started to utilise his home computer and wrote his own industry newsletter, which he sold via the Internet. Frank sprang into action and started repairing cars from his garage at home and eventually found even more profit when he started buying used cars from auctions and selling them on.

I really do believe, because I have experienced it personally many times and witnessed others doing it even more, that there is pain to go through in gathering seed corn - but as they say in the City, 'No pain, no gain. What?'

Fireman in Gloucester teaches a valuable lesson in seed corn

I met a fireman in Gloucester Massachusetts who had wonderful words on seed corn funding. He was a part time fireman and what he called a full time opportunist. Taking advantage of as many business and investment opportunities as he could and over the years he attracted hundreds of such opportunities. He was of the opinion that seed corn was not just a secret of his success but also THE secret. He expanded even further. His belief was that not only must you gather seed corn, but be prepared to get out there and rough it all over again should you lose your seed corn. That was the key. To keep getting it, no matter what the cost and keep investing it, even when times were tough. Getting seed corn and losing it and then quitting was not an option.

Labour intensive activity will bring rewards

Those engaging in the quest for seed corn are advised to take on the most lucrative task to get that cash flow coming in as quickly as possible. To my mind it is well worth going through the pain barrier to get that seed corn funding. I have witnessed many hundreds, if not thousands of people do it. They gravitate toward jobs that pull in hard cash and lots of it, knowing all the time it is for a powerful reason. I have seen many a successful female entrepreneur start their careers by waitressing and earning huge tips, croupier work that entails long late hours, but even bigger tips from rich

Arabs from the major gambling Casinos in every major City, table dancing, house cleaning, dish washing. I have seen their male counterparts get out and do labouring on building sites, mini-cabbing, gardening, all sorts of piece work and network marketing, although in their home country they may very well be doctors, chemists, authors or engineers. Seed corn knows no rules or boundaries. Maybe you have a penchant for selling and if you can get out there and do some serious commission only selling it may be only six or twelve months before you have enough seed corn funding to get into business on your own account. Go where the money is and make it yours.

I know one guy who has three ovens at home and bakes speciality breads, flapjacks and sweetmeats and sells them on a daily basis to local cafes, delicatessens and bakeries...he has tremendous cash flow. The first time I met Josh was when he was delivering pancakes to my favourite deli...where I often stop by for a coffee and a bun. The thought that went through my head was just how many shops have products delivered to them from all sort of people who have developed multiple streams of income. Think about it for a minute...all the products in all the stores have to come from somewhere. Ask yourself the question what could you cook, build, create, manufacture and deliver to a retail shop and in doing so add another stream of income to your portfolio. Think about it for more than a minute – cultivate an obsession about it!

I know of a young lady who works as a school teacher, but evenings and weekends she earns good money doing design work on her computer; websites, logos, letterheads, corporate imaging and branding and product design. She has more money than you can poke a stick at and this additional cash flow she carefully parlays up into rental properties that she buys at the right price. Guess who advises her?

Small retail outlets often sustain empires

It never ceases to amaze me, when you get to know the owners of some small businesses, that the business is just a cash flow vehicle for something much bigger and more grandiose. I know numerous fish and chip shop owners that have some ten, twenty and in one case over a hundred rental properties, all bringing in nice incomes and paying off their mortgages. The number of tailors shops, hair-dressing salons, (Vidal Sassoon even turned his into a Brand along the way) newsagents, every type of clothing store you could imagine, bureaux de change, pawnbrokers, second-hand furniture shops, bicycle repair shops, accountancy practices, legal firms, brokerage companies, whose owners use the cash flow to build factories, mail order dynasties, property empires and other very substantial businesses, is legion.

The other point worth hammering home, now I have implanted the idea, you may very well find it easier to cobble together the necessary wherewithal to open up a retail outlet than cobble together seed corn. Many times one can find a few weeks rent and bringing along a few friends who will help you with the business is easier than one can imagine. And by all means use imagination! By that I mean visualise yourself in a shop doing whatever it is that you do best and wait for the subconscious to come up with ideas and plans which it does with unfathomable regularity. For those in doubt read the fabulous 'Turbo Success - How to Reprogram the Human Bio-computer', penned by my good-self, would you believe?

I can hear some readers saying 'Does that mean that in some cases we actually have to set up shop to get seed corn capital? The answer is, 'You have to do whatever it takes! Simple! Simple as that!'

As an exercise, do yourself a favour and start engaging a shopkeeper in conversation about their business. Don't expect them to open up the first time you buy fish and chips, hock your silver or get your bike repaired, but as you get to know people they will talk and they will open up especially if you show you're interested and enthusiastic about business. Get to know what other businesses they are sustaining from the cash flow from the one you are standing in. Like me, I know you'll often be amazed!

The 'Families'

For many years I have had the privilege to work with and be mentored by many 'ethnic' groups. These could be (in the UK or USA) Jewish, Irish, Indian, Chinese, or any group that are living and working away from their traditional homeland. What they all seem to have in common is that they tend to support each other with a philosophy towards making money that enables them to survive, even in adverse conditions in an alien culture. Many of these philosophies are useful to us if we are to survive and flourish in a business environment where we are possibly trying to start a business with little or no resources. These are the 'families' I refer to in future sections of this book.

Triple power play

Often as not, people are not motivated because they cannot see how small businesses and menial tasks can turn into huge fortunes, so they fail to make the first move. The 'families' on the other hand appear to have an innate understanding that many times you have to leverage small amounts of money into massive wealth and quite often that entails taking the profit from one business and using in another to parlay into a fortune. Over a period of thirty years I have watched my mate E-Type Eddie parlay the sales of second hand motorcycles and cars up in to a substantial rental property empire, the jewel in the crown of which is a 60 acre farm and equestrian centre, right in the heart of the Surrey stockbroker belt. He then snowballed the property empire into a Share portfolio and was recently written up as the country's most successful investor with a picture of him posing in front of his three E-Types and his Lamborghini lurking in the background. A lot of water has gone under the bridge since Eddie and I used our local car park as a car sales showroom!

Gerald Manly had a small racing pigeon business. The cash flow and profits from this allowed him to open a small retail outlet selling pets and the cash flow and profit from the pet shop sustained a property empire of some 40 rental properties and the cash flow and profits from the property business were parlayed into buying unquoted securities, which made him a large fortune. It is all about leveraging whatever asset or cash flow you have, into something bigger and better. As Aristotle once said "If you give me a long enough lever I can move the earth." The secret is to begin something, overcome the problems on a daily basis and keep on solving the problems until you arrive. Once you have arrived, you still have to keep overcoming the problems but at least you can do so with a sense of pride not a sense of desperation.

Eye of the tiger or diversify?

I am a great believer in the fact that there are as many success formulas as there are people and once you have unlocked your own bio-computer and have discovered your own success formula, stick to it, and milk it for all it's worth. I have talked to all sorts of individuals, money grabbers, salesmen, entrepreneurs, businessmen and they all have a story to tell. Some swear blind that what works for them is just sticking at one thing - eye of the tiger - FOCUS...an equal number of people tell me they love to multi-task and the more they have on the go the more money floods in and in actual fact synergies begin to happen within all the diverse opportunities.

50% of a business just for the talking

I have managed to become partner to many businesses, in some cases a fifty-fifty partner, just by talking. Obviously I built a rapport and convinced business owners of my credibility and what I could bring to the party. I always base my deals on the premise that at the moment you have 100% of nothing. 'With my input, sales and marketing ability and my business acumen we can turn this whole thing around and make a small fortune. Do you want me as your partner and together we'll get rich.' Not a bad ploy if you desperately want to get into business but don't have the money but have energy, sales ability or some other skill or attribute to bring to the party. Maybe you have a database, energy, sales enthusiasm, contacts or industry knowledge. This is a deal you can really go, for but don't expect something for nothing!

Talk and grow rich

Every week thousands of people launch into business on their own account. Invariably these people have the same problems as others; lack of capital, domestic problems, full time jobs, bills to pay, commitments to keep, no support, no partner, pressures coming from all sorts of quarters as well as having to overcome past failures, previous debts, a lack of confidence. The difference is they bite the bullet, throw all caution to the wind and jump off the precipice, whether they are ready or not. To their surprise they usually find very quickly that they can fly and suddenly their subconscious minds start to deliver all sorts of creative solutions to problems they would never have thought of consciously. Others have reached a point in their lives of sheer desperation, don't give damn, getting too old for this, last chance, and just do it. And you know what. It works out fine and they wonder why they didn't do it sooner.

Many budding entrepreneurs find they can start generating an immediate income by offering a service that there is a demand for. Maybe you should consider one of the following or at least be stimulated by the list, enough to do your own research and find something that you have aptitude for. I personally know many individuals making serious money carrying out the following services; bereavement counselling, pregnancy counselling, drug and alcohol abuse counselling, marriage guidance, mediators, career guidance, business consultancy, marketing consultancy, teaching meditation, motivational consultancy, sales training, tele-sales training, hypnosis for smoking and weight loss, tarot cards, palmistry and match making. I am convinced the key to success in all of these areas, is starting whether you are ready or not.

No humping heavy stock

Businesses that can generate big fees and commissions just for bringing buyers and sellers together can create wealth with low overheads. The beauty of the business is that it is strictly a paperwork exercise involving no humping stock or manual work. This is a thinking man's business and the larger the stakes the more thought has to go into irrevocable letters of agreement stating the terms and non-circumvention clauses.

Fortunes have been made from commercial real estate, broking planes, heavy engineering equipment, yachts, helicopters, marine equipment, industrial plant and machinery. Brokerages and commission sales can be extremely lucrative. In many instances a one-off deal will give you seed corn funding to start your own portfolio or business. One of the best ways of getting into this kind of businesses is skimming adverts in industrial magazines and newsletters for ideas and see what grabs your attention. I have actually used this method and have been in receipt of funds within 24 hours of picking up a magazine and bringing two parties together using the telephone as the only tool, so I know it works. I made sure that funds were paid into my lawyers client account and the two parties never even met each other until the deal was consummated.

Company starts with £10k OPM, now turns over half a billion pounds

Richard Desmond is the boss of Northern and Shell, a company that turns over some half a billion pounds a year. It was started with *Other People's Money*; £10,000 that, despite initial reluctance, and after a long persuasive lunch, came from Mr Green a music industry mogul. Richard Desmond has a sense of thrift, moral fibre, leads a fantastic family life, is one of those people that lives a Chutzpah business philosophy, is full of charismatic brass neck that he still uses every day in business and once gave me, personally, some tremendous business advice. When I asked Richard what I could do for him, he answered "send me a cigar on my birthday", which I did! The late Anita Roddick talked her neighbour into coming up with £4,000 seed corn for 50% stake of her Body Shop idea in the early seventies and he jumped at the chance. Now one of the richest people in the UK, he lives a life in luxury while Anita and her husband travelled the world, selling franchises, looking for products and having lots of fun.

Families come together

Something you must explore is your own family and nearest and dearest and sometimes those not so near and not so dear. You owe it to yourself and your family to get that seed corn at all costs and overcoming embarrassment and call-reluctance is all part of life's rich tapestry.

Start by listing out all the people in your family tree, even those you haven't seen for years. Obviously start with your Mum and Dad. You never know where loyalties lie and you may strike lucky with long forgotten aunts, uncles, nieces and cousins. All you need is a foot in the door and start talking. Blood is thicker than water and many times you will be able to get outright gifts as opposed to loans. But either way, get the money! What makes it all worthwhile is that the rewards so outweigh any temporary pain, embarrassment and discomfort, it is worth doing a hundred times over.

Moonlighting interviews

Because I love talking to people I find it very easy to engage people in conversation and because of the amount of travelling I do and the weird hours I tend to keep I often find myself talking to people in all sorts of situations, day and night, up and down the country. I talk to bar tenders, bouncers, petrol pump attendants, lorry drivers, mini-cabbers, waiters, office cleaners, night watchmen, security guards. Obviously I can't say that to a man every one of them is earning extra income for seed corn funding. Of course they are not. For many of them this is their only source of income. Others are moonlighting to pay off heavy credit card commitments and other debts that they have incurred through blatant over spending. But many people I have engaged in conversation with are on the trail of seed corn funding to enable themselves to start up their own business, I hope maybe due to encouragement found in my many books and tapes programmes urging people to start businesses on their own account, attaining happiness and financial freedom along the way.

The saddest words in the world, and I have heard them many times. Don't let this be your downfall. Business and investment opportunities to snowball your tiny bit of seed corn into thousands and then millions abound. Don't fall at the first hurdle that life offers up to all comers; get yourself prepared to move on these exciting opportunities when they present themselves.

Don't allow yourself to be crippled by red tape

Today I notice many a would-be-entrepreneur falls at the first hurdle because of the amount of red tape and bureaucracy and petty officialdom. Again I hammer home the point about immigrants not being able to understand the language but they forge ahead to great success, with astonishing rapidity, in many cases quicker than people who are local inhabitants.

High-tech, low-tech, no-tech

Joseph is rushed off his feet. He offers a service where everywhere he goes and works his magic he gets referrals. His phone rings off the hook and he can't cope with the demand. His T Shirt reads Cash Flow is King, and he has plenty of that. What does he do? He's a computer whiz who sorts out his clients' hardware and software problems. One simple bit of magic that he offers is to clean up hard drives that have a habit of slowing down a computer and starting to do 'thinking' all of their own at the most inappropriate times. I can't think of too many businesses where there are not computers continually crashing, operating at a snail's pace and freezing up. Obviously Joseph knows what he is doing, but he is the first to confess he has had no formal training, only that which he has picked up himself over the years.

Nigel's business is booming. He too is in the computer industry and offers an installation and training service. He helps his clients install their new software and then helps them get trained up to peak efficiency in the shortest space of time. Again he gets passed from client to client, never has to advertise and the cash is rolling.

Frank has found the secret to his success and has generated a seed corn machine and he is now seeking to turn that into a green machine. Franks business is valeting cars for dealers. He travels from dealer to dealer, working hard, polishing, buffing, shining, emptying ash trays, blacking or whitening tyres as the case may be, cleaning cars and their upholstery to keep up their appearances and enabling the dealers to attain maximum price. It is all hard work, good fun and creates cash flow.

What grabs me about these three budding entrepreneurs is that they are going in and out of other people's homes and businesses all day long it and it strikes me that there must be thousands of service industry tasks that need carrying out by people who are keen to work, have skills and will go the extra mile to keep their customers happy. Perhaps there is something you can do, in a service that you have specialised knowledge in or enthusiasm for - that could be the cash generator that will turn your life around.

City bonus types with excess disposable income

Over the years I have witnessed many young professionals fritter away money without a care in the world as though money grows on trees and as if there were no tomorrow. As they say in the City, 'More money than brains. What?' I am also old enough to have seen a goodly number of those professionals, burn out, get the sack, lose their JOB because the company collapses, for one reason or another, and there are many reasons why companies collapse, and what seemed to be a gravy train just doesn't come into the station anymore and their income has dried up completely. By the time this happens they have lost 'whiz kid' status and usually all their money.

The secret of course, if you have a good income, is to spend less time in the bars, on yachts and beaches, fewer holidays every year. For goodness sake no one really needs eight vacations a year, not unless you've really made it big time, and start squirreling some money away for a very serious investment programme that will allow you to live the Life of Reilly once your investments have matured.

Conspicuous consumption

The 'families' intuitively know that behind every item in every shop, behind every advert in every newspaper or magazine is an entrepreneur, an executive, a marketing team who spends hours plotting and planning about exactly how to relieve you of your money. Most people outside the circle fall victim to the billion pound advertising campaigns and a pre-programmed have money burning a hole in their pockets.

Those on the quest for seed corn must do something a little different. The starting point is to develop the 'short arms and deep pocket' syndrome. Leave your money in your pockets and your credit cards at home, or better still cut them in half, unless they are part of your seed corn fund strategy, think about purchases over night, stop the impulse purchases of things that attract your attention and get in the mode of creating products that can be sold, instead of buying them!

Work abroad

I have always stressed to gather up your seed corn, go where the money is. I know many people who have done just that and got a well-paying jobs in Nigeria, or Dubai or America, just to get the money flooding in so they get that grub stake sooner rather than later. I have known others to work the cruise ships and there are all sorts of lucrative employment opportunities out there, if you only ask. These opportunities not only pay *extremely* well and also give you an opportunity to *save*.

Make a start

All too often I see people buy a fantastic book on wealth creation and the first thing they do is tell all their mates about it which is great for the authors, and the second thing they do is go out and buy another book on the same subject. Little do they realise that real knowledge comes from actually doing and you will learn a lot more from real life failures than you even will from books.

It may sound daft but the secret of all secrets is to start. Even if you have to open a building society account and stick £10 in it. This is key and it is also imperative that you actually do it. If you don't like the idea of a Post Office account, use a Building Society account or a Bank account, but do get an account open and start squirreling away little bits and pieces of money. More will come as you start to understand this philosophy and develop your own mind. The more your seed corn fund develops, the more opportunities will present themselves to you. Seed corn is the corner stone of this philosophy and you do need to make provision for it and the mentality that comes with it.

My own severest critic

Having been a successful financial author for nearly thirty years, I tend to be my own severest critic. I have just finished reading the proofs of Chapter One of Chutzpah and my thoughts were 'Am I being naive?'

In an endeavour to answer my own critique, I visualise through all the scenarios of people reading my book on trains, on buses, in the office, at home. I think of their backgrounds and what it is they are trying to accomplish in their own lives, and try to fathom out whether I have delivered workable solutions and a philosophy that will work for them, trying to answer every single question along the way.

I rack my brain, based on thirty years business experience. I ask myself 'Have I missed anything out? Have I probed deep enough? Did I witness someone doing something different that I haven't mentioned here? What did and didn't work for me. Surely it all sounds too simple?'

Then it hit me! Yes! I thought Simple is the word. I am not being naive. It's just those people and 'families' that I have witnessed, worked with, studied at close quarters, read about and actually done deals with all did simple things. Sometimes very simple things, but in many, if not most instances were simple things that people outside the inner circle just do not do.

Chutzpah!

It takes Chutzpah to: work in a foreign country, work below ones station, to say 'no' sometimes to yourself and to your family when it comes to making even small purchases, to change habits that may have been with one for a life time, to start saving small amount of money when you have absolutely no idea of how to turn that little seed corn into a fortune.

But at the end of the day, you may very well find that you have to get out there in the big wide world and do things slightly differently to the ways you have being doing things thus far if you really want to succeed beyond your wildest possible dreams.

If you have Plenty of Capital - Invest it Wisely

So far this report has been primarily aimed at those with limited or no resources. However, we must not count out those who have already made a pile, have lots of equity in their house or have been lucky enough to have bequeathed a nice nest egg. Obviously if you have capital behind you to back up your ideas and plans you will go about things in a totally different manner in order to create multiple streams of income. You may want to invest in rental income property either commercial or domestic dwellings or a combination of both.

1. Make it a firm intention you will do whatever it takes to get seed corn funding in the full knowledge it is the starting point of all riches. Intent, Intent, Intent is the real key to getting seed corn

2. As you build the intent of gathering seed corn, be prepared to investigate the many business and investment opportunities you will attract

3. Executive and Non-executive Directors can be a good source of seed corn if you have your own business or business idea that others can back you in

4. If you have to moonlight to earn seed corn make sure you take on the lucrative jobs

5. Angel investors are a specific breed of business people with money to invest as seed corn...attract as many as you can

6. Push all boundaries, use imagination, get creative, but at all costs get the seed corn!

7. Credit cards, although expensive money, sometimes can give you enough seed corn to get you on your road to millions!

8. History shows there are literally thousands of successful people who started their businesses with other people money. You can do the same!

9. Have a yard sale or car boot sale and turn junk into seed corn

CHAPTER THREE

100 NOT SO SMALL BUSINESS IDEAS

But most can be started for under a tenner!

Introduction

First a confession; there are not one hundred small business ideas in this Publication – there are over a hundred. They are a diverse range of opportunities, reflecting the rich variety of the world of work and business we now live in. What they all have in common is that they are easy to start and the majority can be basically set up for around £10. Expensive advertising is dispensed with in favour of networking, a little bit of legwork and imagination and the virtues of "small is beautiful". Most of these ideas require little or no formal training or skills. Many of our 100 Small Business Ideas can be run part-time and combined to achieve a stimulating and profitable lifestyle. All you need is an independent spirit and a "go-for-it" attitude. So what are you waiting for and never forget - the real reason why they are is to stimulate!

At the boot camp

At our MSI boot camps we do a lot of interactive exercises and the following is a particularly useful one. I always start this bit of the talk by asking the attendees how many of them think it would be useful to talk through a number of the small businesses listed here. I always find it fascinating not only to see very few hands go up but also the look on people's faces... it's like 'Wow, what we paid thousands to be here to listen to small business ideas.... I don't think so!'

But I carry on regardless and say, 'I think you're going find this exercise particularly valuable!'

I then pick at random ten of the ideas cited here and start to dissect them...in each case giving at least one example of how someone set up this kind of business and with a tiny amount of capital, creative thinking and cost effective marketing, turned it into a million pound business. Then we go around the table, each attendee then giving examples of what they have seen people do, good or bad, in that type of business or industry. Everyone has a turn and adds to the whole creative pot. These sessions are very stimulating and of course people start coming up with ideas...not necessarily how they make may make that business happen – but more importantly a business of their own choosing!

Advertising consultant

Start in this game for £10 – who are you kidding! Well no one actually. Ok you're not going to be Saatchi and Saatchi overnight, but then again few can afford their fees and you won't need to charge a fraction of what they do to make money. If you have a little imagination, are interested in businesses and what makes people tick, then you've got what it takes to help promote others. Contact start-up firms and offer to chat with them about where they want to go and who they want to reach. Discuss the various advertising media options open to them and offer to produce a cost-effective package.

Think up slogans and visual images that will convey a powerful message about their company and plan a six-month campaign for them. Provide them with a breakdown of costs, including your fee, and get their approval and a first instalment. With your first client you'll be learning all the way, so don't try to have all the answers. Stress that your approach is creative, and offer solutions and new ways of thinking rather than just 'putting an ad in the paper'. Generate excitement about their business and it will become infectious.

After-dinner speaking

If you're a sporting legend, TV star or politician you'll find it easy enough to sign up with an agency and earn handsome fees for telling jokes and anecdotes at conferences and dinners. But most of us are none of these things. However, you may still have experiences that people want to hear about. Have you travelled to unusual places or worked abroad for any length of time, or done an unusual job? Perhaps you're an ex-policeman or fire fighter, a retired vet or serviceman. Do you have an exciting or unusual hobby – sailing, climbing, hot-air ballooning? Perhaps you worked on the QE2 or at the London Hilton, if so who did you meet? Maybe you are an authority on a particular historical period or subject. Whatever your stories, if you can engage an audience with them for twenty minutes or more, you are ready to take bookings from social and Rotary clubs, staff associations, Inner Wheel groups, Women's Institute branches, colleges and schools. Write to the secretaries personally, describing your topic and offering to match your fee to their budget.

Air conditioning

As global warming brings us hotter and longer summers, offices without air conditioning are getting more and more uncomfortable. Installing a permanent system can be prohibitive in terms of cost, and so many firms are looking for a temporary solution as and when required. If you can deliver mobile air conditioning systems and fans to offices within hours of their desperate, sweaty phone call you'll be looked on as something of a lifesaver. Come the beginning of May drop your cards in those older office buildings that appear not have built-in air-con. You may find they'll book some equipment in advance of the heat, meaning you can take a deposit from them and buy or lease what you need. You could easily combine this with delivering bottled water or those big water-cooler fountains.

Aerial photography agent

If you've got your own plane you can take the pictures yourself of course. If not, don't worry. Just contact your nearest small airfield and find out which light aircraft owners offer, or would like to, aerial pictures of the vicinity. Ask them to take a whole range of shots of the surrounding area, getting in as many houses and landmarks as possible. You can then offer these around to any householders or others whose homes or premises appear in the pictures. Give them the option of a blow-up to provide a more detailed view of their own property, or the whole overall picture of their environs. Having such a picture on one's wall is always a talking point. An interesting, unusual and enjoyable small business, which may also bring you commissions for other pictures.

Antique dealing

You can make money from antiques in a number of ways. A lot of people now deal on e-bay and other Internet sites. Having a shop or stall involves outlay, but can still be profitable. Spend some time on research before buying; check out your local auction rooms and clearance sales and get talking to the dealers. Learn about the scams and pitfalls – distressing, fakes, reproductions – and develop an "eye".

A secure outbuilding near a main road can be great for trading in period furniture. Paintings, silver and ornaments are more specialised, but the chance of stumbling on an "old master" or other piece of treasure-trove is always alluring. Buy the Antiques Trade Gazette, which lists weekly auctions all over the country, as well as numerous fairs offering stands from a few pounds for the day.

Art dealing

"I don't know much about art but I know what I like" runs the familiar cry. Individual taste in art is a mystery, and so is the money some people are prepared to pay for it.

This is a speculative business, but unlike other speculations you don't have to risk your own cash to make some. Contact local artists and say you're hosting a "private view" at your house. If they can each bring a bottle of wine you'll hang their pictures on your living room wall and invite business people for drinks and canapés (a dish of olives and some mini-pizzas to you and me). For any works sold on the night you will receive a 10% commission. You could ask more, but this might run the risk of alienating your artists and encouraging them to later sell direct to the punters you've brought along. If your own home is not a suitable venue, look for a trendy wine-bar to host your evenings.

Baby equipment

This stuff can be expensive, and unless one has friends in need it's either a case of storing it all till the next infant arrives or trying to sell it via the local paper. If people can get a reasonable cash price from you for their baths, baby-walkers, slings, papooses, pushchairs, cots etc. they'll beat a path to your door. Baby items are used for such short periods they don't really wear out, so you can sell them on at below new prices, yet still make yourself a profit. Advertise in playgroups, nurseries and among friends. See Child-minding.

Book finding service

If you like browsing in old bookshops there's a simple way you could earn some cash at the same time. For every out-of-print book – and most of the stock in second-hand shops is – there's likely to be someone, somewhere, looking for a copy of it. If you can connect these books to the people who want them you can charge a handsome premium, sometimes far more than the marked price. Advertising in the literary press is costly, so circulate some simple leaflets around colleges – 'Book Search - if not found - no fee' etc. Maintain a list of required titles as you tour the second-hand shops. Quote your own price to your client before making the purchase, unless you know the book is in hot demand. The Internet is ultimately the best way to operate a book-finding service, allowing you to ply your trade worldwide.

Bricklaying

You may not be strictly speaking, a professional "trowel". If however you've laid a few bricks to make a flowerbed or built a decent garden wall at home, then there's no reason you can't utilise this skill to earn money. The more established builders have bigger fish to fry and often don't want to take on relatively minor work. So stress in your advert "Smaller Jobs Welcomed". For garden brickwork you may be able to get away with a rustic look – i.e. wobbly lines and lumpy mortar – but for a garage or extension you'll need to produce an even finish all round. So use your line and level scrupulously if you don't want to get known as a cowboy. Check out the different ornamental blocks now available for building walls and outdoor screens. Arches over gates are also popular, where you first make a plywood template for the shape and build over it. See also Pointing and Gardening.

Cake decorating

If you have a steady hand and can use an icing syringe this is an easy way to earn some money. You don't have to make the cakes, unless you want to, in which case you add it to the customer's bill. The important bit is personalising the cake with what's on top. Ok there's Batman, Britney and Golf-Lovers' cakes available in supermarkets, but what you'll offer is a totally unique message and design. Talk to the client about who the cake's for and what they are into – cars, football, tennis or whatever, and see what you can come up with - the more dramatic or off-the-wall the better, usually. The important thing is it'll be different, a one-off, so think of a name for your business that reflects this – 'Takes the Cake' or 'Cake That!'. Don't forget to photograph each cake you decorate, so you can build a brochure to show new customers.

Candle making

This has been a popular craft activity for many years, with all manner of moulds and kits available from hobby suppliers. It's not only the "new age" crowd who like candles. Candlelight has a unique magic, transforming the blandest dining room into a romantic bistro, fairy grotto or gothic castle. If you have the skills to create your own original designs, that's great. The range of rubber mould kits available however is vast, covering everything from Lord of the Rings chess sets to Elvis. Plain fat altar candles are probably the biggest seller of all among the chic dinner party set. Take a stall at a Craft Fair or offer to New Age and other shops. Look into supplying wrought iron and other types of candle holder to supplement this business. Of course the fantastic thing about making candles for profit is that people burn them and come back to buy more!

Car repairs

Are you good under the bonnet? Got a nice big tool box? Then there's little else you need to start earning money straight away at this game. Almost everyone has a car and at some point something goes wrong with it. Many people are wary of taking their motor to a big garage, fearing they may be ripped off. If you're an honest, straight-talking and competent mechanic who arrives promptly when called out, you'll be a godsend to the motorists in your area. One card in the newsagent's window should be all it takes to get your first customer. Your reputation will take care of the rest.

Caravan maintenance

There are thousands of sited caravans in the UK and the number is growing. The attractions of the caravan as a holiday home, together with the option of rental income means that a growing number of people of all ages are investing in them. Approach the park proprietors and individual owners, offering cleaning and repairs. Valuable services include: repainting, particularly chassis and sub-frames which, in coastal areas are vulnerable to salt-air corrosion – replacing rubber seals around windows and doors – cleaning and checking vans in between lets – tending flower beds and lawns.

Caricaturist

This is all about capturing that indefinable essence of a person in a few strokes of a pencil. Formally trained artists don't necessarily make the best caricaturists. If you've done any cartooning for fun or are just a natural doodler, think seriously about developing the skill. Start observing people's faces and figures, looking for their visual "signature" and try out a few lines. Practice, practice and more practice is the key to drawing ability, and with caricaturing, simplicity and a light touch are also integral. So gather a few willing subjects and get sketching. When you feel ready, advertise for appearances at private functions and dinners. People (hopefully!) won't expect to be flattered by a caricature of them-selves. What they will enjoy is seeing their partners, friends and colleagues given the comic treatment.

Carpet cleaning

After the extended fling with wood laminate flooring, homeowners are resuming their passionate love affair with carpet. It's cosier, quieter, warmer and much nicer to lie on in front of a roaring fire and – well, relax... But carpets always need cleaning on a regular basis and it's not a task the average homeowner is geared up for. If you don't want to splash out on buying your own specialist equipment straight away, then punt around for your first job and rent a carpet cleaner. Suppliers will give you advice on how to use their products, and after that it's just common sense. Obviously price each job according to size, and suggest reasonable discounts to groups of neighbours if you can visit them on the same day. Leaflet offices, pubs and shops as well as the residential market.

Car valeting

The time when suburban man spent Sunday mornings lovingly washing his car seems long gone. Nowadays he's too busy visiting the DIY superstore and eating out at his local gastro-pub. This is where you come in. Offer a range of services, from basic washing to full luxury valet – waxing and polishing the bodywork, trim and mirrors, vacuuming and cleaning the interior, including upholstery, dashboard, windows, even the furry dice and nodding dog if any! Seriously though, this is a good cash earner, with regular repeat business, especially if you can collect and return vehicles at the owners' convenience. Don't forget those little extras like a spray of fragrance before you hand the keys back. You could also leave a complimentary air-freshener on the driver's mirror. As well as private motorists, approach fleet hire firms and companies with their own executive vehicles.

Catering

Ever been to a party and thought you could make a better job of the food? If so, why not have a go at outside catering. You can start on your own providing cold buffets for family events or office meetings, building up to wedding parties of hundreds of guests. Food regulations don't insist you have special premises, but if you cook professionally at home you must still fulfil hygiene requirements and are liable to inspection. To optimise profits, don't forget to source your ingredients at wholesale prices wherever possible. Organic food is increasingly preferred and you could attract a lot of business by offering this option. There is also a growing fashion for having an outsider come in and prepare a gourmet dinner party in one's own home. This usually means you can use the client's own kitchen and equipment on site. If you have a flair for food - and like to chat about it – this might be an enjoyable enterprise to explore. Don't forget the big white hat – always look the part.

Cattery

If you're a cat lover yourself you'll be a natural at this. You'll need suitable accommodation of course, as befits this most lordly of pets. Ask about any special dietary requirements before the owners leave their cats with you, also things like injection status and whether toms have been "done". Otherwise you might find yourself with a lot more furry little guests than you started out with! Holiday months are obviously going to be busiest, but if you can get some frequent flying executives to entrust their cats to you on an equally frequent basis it'll help keep your occupancy rates up throughout the year.

Child minding

Childcare can be a problem for working parents and private nurseries can stretch resources. If you've had children of your own you'll probably have all the basic experience. Usually the parents will drop off their children and collect them at the end of the day, though you could offer to collect them if you have child safety seats in your car. Charge either by the day (and clarify how long a "day" is) or the hour and if you are supplying meals ask about any special dietary requirements for the children.

Traditionally child-minding has been an ad hoc business with informal arrangements between parents and minders. You should however contact your local authority for details of how to become a registered child-minder.

Chimney sweep

If you've always fancied yourself as a bit of a Dick Van Dyke dancing around the chimney pots, why not take up this time-honoured trade. Ok, a lot of people have central heating now, but real fires and stoves are much valued for the cheery glow they give to a living room. The ready availability of smokeless fuel means there's no restriction on using chimneys, which will need regular sweeping to remove both soot from the fire and debris building up from above. This is a messy job, so be prepared to wear a sooty face, customers will be disappointed with anything less! You'll need the classic set of brushes and rods, a special vacuum cleaner and protective sheets to fit tightly around the fireplace. Children love to run outside and see the brush pop out the chimney pot, and you may often find yourself photographed. That sooty face is therefore obviously an asset, and if you're also a "bit of a character" you'll find your services much sought-after. It's also considered good luck to have the chimney swept before getting married and some couples ask the sweep to attend their wedding. You might like to get an old-fashioned costume to wear on these occasions. Contact the National Association of Chimney Sweeps for advice. Oh, and watch "Mary Poppins" for the dance routines...

Cleaning supplies

In the States, men selling household cleaning materials were a familiar feature of life in the 1950s. You can knock on doors if you like with this business, but you might find it easier to leave a simple list of your supplies in letterboxes and allow householders to phone their orders through to you. With supermarkets offering deliveries online these days you'll need to have a unique selling point. Shop around for the right wholesaler and ask for an account. Then offer discounts on detergents, bleach, sprays, polishes, cloths, dusters, scourers, vacuum cleaner bags, mops and mop-heads. Approach social clubs and staff associations, where people can club together and place a large order with you. See Office Cleaning and Domestic Cleaning.

Clown

No don't laugh, clowning is a serious business. That's not to say you won't *have* a great laugh most of the time. "But don't I need to learn juggling, or stilt-walking?"

If you're going to do street entertaining then yes, you'll probably need circus skills.

But there's a big demand for kids' birthday party entertainers, where some fluffy puppets, simple magic tricks and balloon modelling are always popular. Buy or make a colourful costume, get some face paints and work on a routine; the simplest things work best, visual gags – contorting your face and body into funny shapes, a silly voice and cracker-jokes rarely fail. Remember that kids, though charming, can be hard work, and their attention spans, thanks to TV and computers, are not what they used to be. Have a varied programme and move quickly on to the next trick if the audience loses interest. Stress that parents/hosts must remain present to supervise. This is definitely a job you'll get better at with experience, learning from the different responses of the children. Clowning will keep you on your toes, but once you get a good reputation, it'll also keep money coming in. According to demand, look to charge between £75 and £100 for a one hour show.

Coin dealing

The proper word for coin collecting is "numismatics". Not a lot of people know that. But people do make a lot of money out of coins. As with all collectibles, knowledge is the crucial factor. Age however does not necessarily imply greater value. Roman coins for example are two a penny, kind of, whereas a 19th century one-cent coin fetched $100,000 at auction. Some people buy special editions and keep them in sealed plastic folders – condition can dramatically affect a coin's worth – others stick to a particular historical period or country and learn everything there is to know about it. Visit coin fairs and dealers, including the legendary Spinks, and start learning yourself. Take any interesting coins of your own around and see what people will offer. As your knowledge grows, exhibit at the collectors' fairs and you'll soon be coining it yourself.

Computer and telephone cleaning

This is a B2B (business to business) service which you can quickly build into a profitable enterprise. Computers, hand-held mice, and telephone receivers in particular are used by multiple employees a minimum of eight hours a day. By the end of the week they are greasy, grimy, sweaty and unpleasant to use. And that's just the employees! Seriously though, office equipment needs to be regularly cleaned and freshened up. Cleaning suppliers can advise you on some specialist anti-static cloths and sprays, and your job will be to visit firms on a weekly or monthly basis, ensuring that all their screens, phones, work-stations, copiers etc. are sweet and fragrant for the staff to use. This is a very simple business to start and operate. See Office Cleaning.

Computer training

You don't have to be a high-flying technology geek to teach people how to use a computer. The fact you've accessed this material means you already have sufficient knowledge to pass on. Kids learn I.T. at school these days, but for many of the over-forties generation, computers are still a mystery. More and more of our everyday needs are being processed online - information, banking, shopping, booking tickets etc. Unable to use a computer, a lot of older folk are feeling increasingly isolated and frustrated as a result. Many would also love to take advantage of email to stay in touch with relatives and friends abroad. What they want is someone who can show them the basics of getting an email address, mailing, website access and using search engines. If you can do this in a friendly, jargon-free way, you'll be welcomed with open arms.

Advertise in your local library and community centre, offering one-to-one tuition or small groups. Do home visits or hire a small room if you get a big response. Remember your potential clients may not even own a PC yet, and a computer store can be a bewildering place for the novice, so offer to talk through the different options with them. As the grey revolution marches on, your "silver surfers" will be riding along on the crest of the wave!

Cookery classes

People will sign up for these as much for the social aspect as what they expect to learn. Obviously you'll need to be able to cook yourself, and if you have a passion for creating mouth-watering dishes you'll be sure to get people fired up. Start at home if you've a big enough kitchen and equipment. You provide the ingredients and wine for everyone and get your students to participate in the preparation. Have some nice music on as you work and talk them step-by-step through each dish. Finally you all sit down to eat. Either charge for a series of evenings, or per night. Base your fee on what they'd pay for a comparable meal and drinks at a restaurant. For each session print hand-outs with the full recipe and background notes. Bon appetite!

Craft fairs

Hire out a small hall or room above a pub on a Saturday or Sunday. Offer arts and craft people the hire of a table to sell their wares. Distribute posters and leaflets and advertise in the local paper. Your earnings will be the differential between your spend on the hall and advertising, and the table-hire from your craftspeople. Don't expect an instant profit. It may take a few weeks to build up business. If using a pub which wants to attract more drinkers, you may be able to get the room for free. Consider a nominal charge of say 50p on the door for customers. If they've paid to come in, it may make them more inclined to buy something and make the 50p investment worthwhile. This will keep your exhibitors happy enough to book a regular pitch. Crafty!

Curtain making

This is rather like being a bespoke tailor for people's windows. One can buy ready-made curtains in all sizes, but usually in a limited range of prints. Do your leafleting and then approach fabric shops, tell them you're a curtain maker and ask if they can loan you swatches to show prospective clients. Alternatively, get the fabric shops to refer you to their customers and you do the same for them. Be sure to carefully measure both windows and fabric, and discuss the all-important "drop" with your clients. See Interior Design.

Decorating

Suggesting home decorating as a simple business might seem like teaching your grandmother to suck eggs, but as granny would also say "don't knock it!" Houses always need painting, inside and out. True, there are plenty of people already in this game, but if you do a nice, clean job at reasonable prices you'll always be in demand.

Estimating is a tricky business, but don't be tempted to put too low a price in just to get the work. Ask customers to buy or choose the paint, to make sure they like the colours. Remind them that charts can be deceptive and the effect of a particular colour when it's on their walls might surprise them. Word of mouth is, as always the best source of new business, but to start out, drop leaflets and place some cards in newsagents' windows.

Dog grooming

You can either conduct this business in your own "Poodle Parlour" home or shop premises, or visit clients at their home (or kennel!) Put a card up at your local vet's.

Also talk to the owners of your nearest pet shop. Maybe, if they have a corner out back, you could make an arrangement to come in one or more days a week to give canine trims. Get to know the names (and temperaments!) of your regulars and take an interest in them. It will all help build up your client base. Dog Grooming is obviously an ideal business to combine with the one below.

Dog walking

Love animals? Always been a "doggie person"? If so, and you've time on your hands when busy pet owners in your neighbourhood haven't, then this could be the perfect profitable business for you. If you think it's "a walk in the park" you'd be right, up to a point! If you have your own faithful pooch that you love to bits, do remember that other people's dogs may not be quite as cuddly or well behaved. The way you're going to make good money from this service is by simple multiplication; two, three, four, maybe even half a dozen canine cuties if you think you can handle them (and a "pooper scooper" as required!) If you're patient and reliable, have some open space nearby and are prepared to go out in all weathers (dogs need exercise come rain or shine) then go out and "fetch" your first customer. Good boy!

Dolls houses

If you're a bit of a hobbyist and "detail freak" you'll find this an extremely satisfying business. There is a strong nostalgia market for individually made items like these, and doting parents, grandparents, aunts and uncles are prepared to pay good prices for lovingly constructed dolls houses. This can be a wonderfully creative husband and wife activity – one assembling the houses, the other the tiny furniture. You can sell your houses either furnished or unfurnished, and provide a catalogue of your own dolls-house fittings for additional sales. Your finished product will be your best advertisement, so don't forget to put a little permanent label with your phone number somewhere in each house so that admiring relatives and friends can order their own. So clear out the spare room, get the radio and the tea on and prepare for the Christmas rush! See Wooden Toys.

Domestic cleaning

Forget the Mrs Mop image, domestic cleaning is now a massive market and a good source of income for both men and women. Many people simply haven't the time or energy to do their own chores and are delighted to pay others for the privilege. Apart from expecting you to do a thorough job, clients will need to feel they can trust you, as you'll probably have the run of their house while they're at work. So put your full name and address and offer references on all your advertising. The work itself is fairly self-explanatory – vacuuming, washing up, floor mopping, bathroom and kitchen cleaning – whatever the customer wants done. An hourly rate is usual, so check out the local competition. Most households will want you once or maybe twice a week. To boost your earnings aim to consolidate your customer base within particular areas on the same day, thus cutting out travelling time between jobs.

Drain clearance

This is one of those unpleasant jobs that no one wants to do. Well, not unless they're getting paid for it, which you will be. Sinks, outside drains and yes, toilets will all become grist to your mill in the wonderful world of drain clearance. Sometimes all you'll need is a firm pull on your plunger to get things running away, other times you'll have your sleeves rolled up to the elbow and beyond and the job will be very much hands on! Read up on basic plumbing and if you stress "emergency availability" on your leaflets be prepared for out of hours calls too. Later on invest in a set of drain rods and if you want to be really high-tech, a fibre optic camera you can feed down the pipes to diagnose the source of the blockage.

Draught proofing

Leaflet older houses with an imaginatively designed advert - a Jack Frost cartoon character trying unsuccessfully to get in a window, thwarted by the draught-proofing while the homeowners sit warm and cosy by the fire. You get the picture? The draught-proofing material you'll need is a simple narrow plastic strip. One side is furry the other has a peel-off backing which leaves an adhesive surface. You access the windows and doors where the edges meet the frames and attach the draught-proof strip all the way along, thereby keeping the cold air out. Get your draught-proof strip from any DIY store and plan a big ad campaign from September on.

English tuition for foreigners

People of all nationalities want to learn English, as it's a passport to international success. EFL (English as a Foreign Language) schools in this country bring young students over all year round and provide intensive training and sometimes accommodation too. It isn't essential to have a degree or formal training to make a good living in this game, either teaching one-to-one or setting up your own school.

Some TEFL courses (which train people to teach EFL) are expensive so shop around and do some research before signing up for one. If you're the "teach yourself" type buy some specialist books on EFL and study the techniques. There's a big emphasis on grammar, and you'll be surprised how eager non-native speakers are to grasp the formal elements of English. They'll usually want to study for the various "Cambridge" exams, as these help with job applications. There are plenty of standard workbooks which cover these courses, so students can study with you and enter the examinations independently.

Entertainment agent

This can be anything from hiring out people for kids' parties (see Magician and Clown) to booking celebrities to speak at Rotary Clubs and Corporate functions, (See After-Dinner Speaking) or even signing Rod Stewart for a world tour. Go to see bands, singers, magicians, comedians and speakers and get hold of their publicity material. Then talk to club and pub secretaries and owners about bookings. Make sure your entertainers are reliable and obviously that they are entertaining! Deal straightforwardly with artists, and pay out as soon as you receive your fees. Contact the Entertainment Agents Association for advice on charges and other legal aspects.

Escort service

This term is still used as a euphemism for call-girl businesses, but there are actually some very practical reasons why escorts, male and female, are in demand. There are now an increasing number of women in business and the professions. When required to attend formal occasions and corporate dinners where convention expects them to bring a partner, they may require a presentable male to fulfil this role for the evening.

Usually no pretence is required, just the ability to wear a dinner suit, eat a meal and make pleasant small talk for a couple of hours. Oh, and accept an agreed fee for your efforts. Nice work if you can get it. It is still likewise assumed that professional men will attend such events with a female companion. For obvious reasons a lot of actors and actresses make a good part-time income from legitimate escort work. But you don't have to be especially sophisticated in any way, just prepared to look and act the part, blend in and make up the numbers. If you're a reasonable dancer this might be a fact worth advertising. Whether male or female be prepared for occasional sexual overtures and risqué invitations, and whatever your feelings in the matter, take care how you deal with them. You can either register with an agency for this sort of work, or advertise yourself. Better still, start your own agency.

Fancy dress hire

You will need to make an investment here, either buying a range of basic outfits or running them up yourself if you can use a sewing machine. Your main business will be from "theme" parties and these tend to be things like "Wild West" "Sixties" "Elvis" and "Tarts & Vicars" as well as the usual Halloween, Christmas and Valentine's Night occasions. Check out party supplies companies for costumes and celebrity masks. It might be easier to simply sell these on, especially to corporate clients who have budgets for team-building and other staff events. Hold a deposit on all hired items and remember they'll need washing each time. A large spare room at home might work for this business; if you do lease a shop you can sell other party items – cards, balloons, confetti, tableware etc., to boost your takings.

Fencing

Not the Errol Flynn kind, but the garden fence kind. All the materials are available at your local DIY superstore or garden centre – every type of larch lap, lattice wood, feather-edged, you name it they've got it these days. Just ascertain exactly what your customer wants and work out how many sections and posts will be required. You'll also need cement for setting the posts and it's important these are securely positioned.

Obviously the usual tools for fixing everything together, including the all-important spirit level! When the job's complete, offer to come back each year and re-creosote the fence, or paint it with one of the environmentally friendly products now available.

Flat-pack furniture assembly

People buy flat-pack furniture because they think it's easy and hassle-free to put together. That is, until they open the box and look at the instructions. These minute diagrams – often a maze of arrows, numbers and worded in eight languages – can be enough to drive the sanest person to tearing their hair out. If you can transform the disjointed contents of their cardboard box into a hallstand, bookcase, cabinet or whatever it is they thought they were buying, the purchasers of these objects will gladly pay you for the time and grief you save them. Put up your card "Flat-Pack Furniture Assembled" in all the DIY stores. Sorted!

Floor sanding

There's many thousands of Victorian, Edwardian and later period houses with splendid, solid, knotty old floorboards. To the connoisseur homeowner these are "the real thing" and laminates simply don't compare. If these floorboards have lain under carpets for decades they'll need sanding down to bring up the grain, then sealing and waxing to a shade of the owner's choice. Sanding floors is both noisy and *very* dusty. Protect your own lungs with a proper mask and the client's furnishings with dustsheets and tape across the doorframes while you're working. Alternatively use an industrial sanding machine with a vacuum bag attachment. Carry a specially curved floorboard saw to remove broken timbers and carry out repairs.

Football memorabilia

If you know what you're doing you can make some serious money at this. Autographed items are the most sought-after and those from the more legendary games can be gold dust. Why not dust off some of the items in your own attic, have a spin round the Internet and see what's hot. You may not have a "Boys of '66" mint condition programme, but you'll be surprised at the kind of soccer-related things people collect – press clippings, rare recordings of interviews, scarves, rosettes, photographs. The smart cookies treat this business as a long-term investment activity – today's discarded plastic toy can be tomorrow's priceless souvenir.

Freelance press photographer

This is not as much of a closed shop as many people imagine. It's very much an opportunist's business – both actively looking for those opportunities and snapping them ruthlessly when they unexpectedly come to you. Any lunchtime outside London's Ivy restaurant you can see the paparazzi hovering on the chance of spotting a star arrive or leave, and they're not usually disappointed. Admittedly photos of celebrities can command the highest prices from magazines and newspapers, but shots of dramatic events can also be very saleable – lightning striking a tree, a huge wave washing up over a street, a tall chimney being demolished and of course, scenes of accidents and disasters. Speed is often of the essence with a hot photo, and having a digital camera enabling you to send the picture online anywhere in the world will prove a huge advantage. You can either contact publications direct to sell your pictures or offer them through a syndicate or press agency.

French polishing

This is one of those "dying arts". Treasured items of furniture, pianos, doors and panelling all suffer scratch marks and need restoring. French polishing tends to have an aura of mystique, but there's no big secret or major training required. You'll need to find the professional stains and waxes and create the exact match on the wood and learn how to apply the successive layers to achieve that rich finish. A good eye for colour is also required. If you can knock out your own wooden coffee tables and other bespoke furniture, giving it a real French polish finish will warrant a higher price tag among connoisseurs. Leaflet period properties and consider an advert in the Antiques press.

Gardening

Don't feel you have to have an encyclopaedic knowledge of plants and soil types to get a start in this game. Often as not, your customers will have all the know-how. What they want is someone to do the spadework. Gardens are a bit of a British obsession, and even the simplest back yard needs weeding, pruning and mowing. Get to know people running your local garden centre and leave your card with them. Drop leaflets at any house that looks overgrown – don't assume just because there's a jungle outside they're not bothered, they may have just been putting off the inevitable. Don't splash out on a lot of tools till you know you'll need them. Many householders have a shed full of gear and may be happy for you to use it.

Greeting cards

Ever been surprised how expensive birthday cards can be? And they're all much of a muchness too. All you're buying is cardboard and a print design for £2 sometimes nearer £3. Buy a quantity of cards and experiment with your own designs. You don't need drawing skills. For example, pressed flowers glued on the front can be beautifully impressive. Photocopy pictures from old books where the copyright is long since irrelevant and transfer them to your cards. Sell to art shops, independent gift stores, bookshops and craft retailers.

Gutter maintenance

Mainly this will involve clearing leaves and silt to allow rain to flow freely away. When gutters are blocked water overflows causing inconvenience, damage to the property and ingress into the house. Basic equipment required is a long ladder, preferably with "standaway" attachment to allow you to peer over into the gutter as you work. At certain times of year beware of wasp nests which sometimes appear in build-ups of silt, especially just around the down-pipe. If you do see insects buzzing around protect hands and face and arm yourself with an appropriate proprietary spray. If handy with a screwdriver you can offer to fix any flailing sections of gutter back to the wall and in the case of rusted metal guttering, replace the whole system with plastic.   See Window Cleaning

Home insulation

There are still many houses, particularly older ones, whose lofts are not insulated. The savings this can make in energy bills are indisputable. Drop some leaflets to likely properties and include a rough quote. You'll need the rolls of insulation material, a small ladder and a knife. Wear overalls, gloves, cap and mask to protect you from the fibreglass. If the loft is unlit you'll need lighting and an extension lead. Remember to move carefully on the joists, one slip and you could be in the ceiling repair business before you know it! See Draught-proofing.

Home security consultant

This can range from fitting a lock to the installation of sophisticated alarm systems. If you don't have the skills for either, there are three easy yet extremely effective alternatives you can offer to householders. The first is door chains; these are available from any DIY store and are simple to fit. Then there are eye-spy or pinhole viewers; these allow the householder to see anyone standing on their doorstep without being seen themselves. Drill a single hole, but first check the height of the user – they may not be as tall as you and won't want to stand on a chair every time the doorbell rings! The third security item you can fit in your clients' homes is a set of window bolts. These are specifically for sash windows and consist of two parts; a pair of bolts set flush into each side of the upper frame, into which a second pair of bolts can be screwed as and when required. If you set the bolts an inch or two from where the upper and lower frames meet, the window will then open sufficient for ventilation but no further. When the householder wants to open the window wide, they simply take off the secondary bolts using a special key. For other types of window, appropriate devices are also available to restrict the opening width. Apart from protection from intruders, parents of young children will also welcome these fittings, particularly on upper floor windows, to avoid accidents.

House finding service

There is no legal reason to use an estate agent when buying a house, and many people prefer to avoid the fees and deal directly with the vendor when buying their home. If they have time they trawl the Internet, look out for private small ads and drive around their desired area on the weekends. If they don't have the time, they can come to you, and pay a partial, modest up-front fee to do it all for them. When you notify them about a suitable home and the purchase goes through, they pay the balance of your finder's fee. You can do the same for sellers of course, and both they and the buyer of a particular house may be your clients. So in effect you are an estate agent, but don't get involved in valuing or negotiating. Of course you can also notify buyers of agency-advertised properties, and earn your fee in the same way if the house-hunters are happy with what you find. Local knowledge will be your big asset for would-be buyers from other areas. Advertise in low-cost lineage classifieds.

House sitting

When people are away on holiday or a business trip, the best security for their home, given that surveys reveal burglar alarms going off are frequently ignored, is to have someone living there. Or rather, have it look like someone's there. For the way to make money from house sitting is to have a number of jobs running concurrently. Your service will involve calling in once or twice a day (always varying the times) turn lights on and off, rearrange vases in the window, bring in dustbins, collect post from the mat and generally give your client's home that lived-in look. You may also water plants, feed and tend pets and deal with any emergencies. Offer to do shopping ready for the owner's return, and don't forget a complimentary flourish to welcome them back – a nice card or even some fresh flowers on the table. Trust and reliability are obviously the cornerstones of this business, and a reputation for caring for clients' homes as if they were your own will be your best advertisement.

Image consultant

Sometimes, people who are talented, brainy, clever or whatever, just don't have the right image to make them a success in their chosen field. They've got ability and ambition by the bucketful, but they just come over as a bit of a Wally in the appearance department. This has got nothing to do with their looks, as such it's just the way they present themselves. If you've got a background in fashion, hairdressing, grooming, retail clothing or just have good dress sense, you should consider entering the image consultancy business. Your clients will usually know they have a problem and that's why they'll come to you. Not for a "What Not to Wear" telling off, but for sympathetic and effective remodelling of their appearance. Sometimes it will be the simplest changes that transform a person – a different colour suit, altering the frames of their glasses, a new style of haircut. It takes an impartial, professional outsider to spot where these changes are required. See Life Coach.

Interior design

Once the preserve of debutantes and the art college elite, interior design is now a job anyone with a feel for colour and space can be successful at. Once you've done your first job, referrals will follow. Be prepared to spend time nurturing each client, producing copious sketches, diagrams and suggestions before they decide on a concept and go ahead. Office design is another angle, with some companies changing their décor as often as the hand towels. They often have large budgets and want to create an atmosphere that makes a "statement" about their business. You could also arrange purchases and trades people for both corporate and residential clients. See Personal Shopper and Decorating.

Ironing service

People who work in offices all need their shirts, skirts and tops to be free of creases. In our long-hours culture most of them don't have time for ironing. There are some people who actually enjoy it though. If you're one of them then you've a head start in this business. Whether you're an ironing enthusiast or not, there's plenty of work waiting out there. An d don't forget that, so long as you don't completely lose concentration and end up with singed garments, ironing is one of those calm activities that allows you to listen to the radio or music while you work. You could even have audio recordings on and learn a language as you smooth away. Most clients will expect you to pick up and return their items, so consider investing in an advertising logo on your car or van, so others can take your phone number. How about "Smooth Operator" as a business name?

Jams and preserves

If you grow blackberries, apples, pears, figs, raspberries, gooseberries or other fruits in your garden, you've probably had a go at making jam. When you got fed up eating it yourself you probably gave it away. You may have sold some at your garden gate.

Since the fruit cost you nothing, you probably made a good profit. However, unless you have a vast acreage of berries, you won't have sufficient produce to make even a bread and butter living out of the jam business. And there won't be enough customers passing your garden gate to set you on the road to a fortune either. Not unless you live by the M25, and even then they won't be able to stop. Once you've sold your first few jars and had a good response, think up a quaint name (anything Old English is a good bet) and print nice labels. Offer your jams to health food shops, delicatessens and consider advertising on the Internet for a worldwide market. Oh, and find a market gardener who can supply the big quantities of fruit you're going to need.

Laundering

We're talking about clothes and bedding here not money! You can however make money by doing other people's dirty washing for them. Couples in rented flats in particular may not even have a washing machine, or if they do, the time to use it.

Collect and return each client's items, neatly folded. Ensure things don't get mixed up by using separate labelled bags. You don't want frilly underwear or Yfronts causing any embarrassment among clients! See Ironing and Domestic Cleaning services.

Life coaching

This is still a new profession, imported from America and growing fast here in the UK. At present no formal training or qualifications are required but if you've worked in any kind of training capacity before, or are simply a good communicator, you may well have what it takes to be a life coach. Your clients' needs will vary; some will be looking for practical support – organising their schedules, helping them juggle home and work commitments and focus on other long-term goals. Others may require more personal counselling and emotional guidance. Many will want a bit of both. Read a wide selection of self-help books – psychology, mentoring, educational theory and life-long learning studies – and consider taking a course in one or more of these subjects. Life they say is a rich tapestry, and at the end of the day, it will be your own experiences - problems, challenges, changes and joys – together with an intelligent and sympathetic attitude - that best qualifies you to be a life coach.

Agree a fixed monthly fee and hours with each client, but also expect "crisis" phone calls from them at odd hours; life coaching isn't a nine-to-five job, and if you're good at it you'll be regarded as a bit of a lifeline too.

Local newspaper

People are interested in local news, what's going on in their area. What you'll be interested in is the advertising revenue you can attract from local firms. If you have access to a photocopier and keyboard you can start straight away. Ask every business in your vicinity to advertise with you, stressing the virtue of "keeping things local". Don't worry that your paper may look like a parish magazine at first – this lack of slickness will be its appeal. Established local papers will deal with court reports and crime, so focus your editorial on the upbeat stories – new restaurants and businesses opening – which you can also nurture for advertising sponsorship. Interview prominent people in the area and get them "on side". With persistence, this is a pleasant hobby which can be built into a very profitable business indeed.

Magician

Learning card tricks can take years. But there are also some you can learn in a few minutes. It's the same with other types of illusion. Some require the kind of sleight of hand only seasoned professionals possess, but there are also hundreds of tricks on the market, which are "self-working". Check out magic suppliers on the Internet, get some catalogues and have a look. Read a few books and watch some magic shows and you'll soon realise that conjuring is largely about "patter". This patter, usually comic, both entertains the audience and acts as a diversion while the trick is being worked. Many high-profile magicians wouldn't claim to be highly skilled, but their personality is the real secret of their success. Tommy Cooper started out as a serious magic man and things just kept going wrong. The rest - just like that - is history!

Marriage bureau

Introduction agencies suffer from a somewhat seedy image. Every newspaper and TV channel these days seem to offer a dating service. Working people often find it difficult to meet a potential life-partner and are put off by the rather up-front cattle-market approach of computer matches and speed dating. Why not go back to where it all began, and start up a discreet, civilised and unhurried marriage bureau. Have some tasteful cards printed and visit clients in person. Talk to them informally yet at length and take notes. Charge a registration fee, keep their details on file and make it clear your service is personal and never rushed. Bringing people together who are right for each other is both a great art and a privilege. In a world of instant fixes you will be offering something very special, creating lasting happiness through your skill, understanding and judgement.

Messenger

Contact big and small firms that are likely to send out a lot of packages, either for the post or delivered locally. Give your full details for security purposes and references if possible. Allow clients to call on your mobile any time with their errand and delivery requirements. Maybe they've an urgent package to catch the last post or need some particular stationery items picked up before lunch. Be available for any and every request. In a built-up area a bicycle, moped or even your two feet may be more efficient – and cheaper – than running a car. Businesses will expect you to invoice them each month, so make sure you have some cash flow before commencing. Call yourself Hermes or Mercury – anything that conveys the swiftness of the gods!

Mini-cabbing

This is probably one of the quickest ways to earn some cash, and cab firms especially in big cities are always looking for more drivers. However there's no reason why you can't set up on your own and operate as a one-man band, especially now mobile phones mean you don't need a radio. Check your insurance and any local authority licensing requirements and get some cards printed. As you are a solo operator, make a virtue of this; show your full name and address and think up a slogan, or catchy title for your service, e.g. "Tim's Taxi –

always On Time" or "Charley's Chariot". Weekends are usually busiest, but pub and club work inevitably involves picking up drunks – some of whom may not be as well behaved as others. If you prefer more congenial passengers, there's a growing demand for the daily "school run" with parents concerned to get their children safely to and from the school gates. And if you don't mind being paid monthly by cheque, account work with companies can generate steady income. If you're in the country, commuters need to get to the station; encourage them to leave their own car at home and "save the planet" by letting you drop and collect them, along with two or three others each day. Bus services are lamentably poor in rural areas; get a people carrier and you could soon be providing a very welcome transport option in your area.

Mirror restoration

Antique mirrors can be extremely valuable. But mirrors that have the look and feel of old ones also sell well. Pick up any tatty mirrors going cheap at auctions or boot fairs. Use any basic wood to repair or rebuild the frames. You will need at least one old antique-style frame with those big swirls and whorl shapes. This will be your mould. Cover the frame with Vaseline, then plaster of Paris, pressing it firmly into all the shapes and grooves of the frame. When dry, turn over and lift off your original frame, leaving you with a plaster mould. Vaseline this mould and pour in plaster mixed with PVA or Gesso to make your first new "old" frame. Don't worry if your frames are a bit lumpy or uneven in places, this adds to its period charm. Spray or paint with antique gold or other colours and stick to the wooden mirror frame. You can use the same method to dramatically transform cheap old paintings. Who's the cleverest of them all!

Mobile hairdresser

If you cut hair and/or do sets and perms, leasing a shop is a big expense every month. Cut out this overhead (pun definitely intended) by visiting clients in their own homes or welcoming them to yours. If you opt for the latter you can claim a relevant portion of electricity and mortgage/mortgage payment against tax. Being peripatetic allows you to claim fares or petrol. Beauticians, aroma- therapists, masseuses and reflexology practitioners can all work this way.

Patio cleaning

Over time, paving slabs and garden paths get mottled and stained with lichen and pollutants. The best way to clean them is with a high-pressure water spray. These portable units, which you can hire or purchase, direct a powerful, needle-sharp jet to dissolve away stubborn grime. Lime scale and greasy areas can be treated with lemon juice, vinegar or a proprietary chemical to break down stains prior to using the jet-spray. This is a simple task, which produces pleasing results for the householder. Quote according to the size of the paving area. Advertise on garden centre notice boards. The jet-sprays can also be used to clean brickwork, greenhouses and conservatories.

Office cleaning

This is big business and there are some very large concerns involved in the office cleaning game. So how does a one-man-band go about getting a slice of this multi-million pound industry? Answer: by going for the jobs the big boys don't want to touch, the smaller offices that haven't got the budget they're interested in. Just look around your local area – there will be dozens of smaller firms, estate agents, solicitors, opticians, and retailers, all needing their premises cleaned. Leaflet them all and assure them you're thorough, reliable and like them, a "small-enough-to-care" business and on their doorstep. You can start using your own home vacuum cleaner if you want – that and some dusters and spray polishes for desks and other surfaces is your basic equipment. If you work at this job early mornings can use the rest of the day to pursue other business interests. Or play golf if you want to!

Organic deliveries

Locate your nearest organic farms or wholesalers. Compile a simple leaflet based on what you can source from them and work out your own retail prices, making sure you have a realistic profit margin. Drop your leaflets into likely looking homes and sort out some space in the back of your car while you await your first order. Items in demand will be potatoes and other bulky vegetables, and eggs too, which many non-meat eaters like as a protein substitute. Check out health-food suppliers for nuts, seeds and grains and offer these to your customers too. If your suppliers have Soil Association stamp of approval, add this information to your own publicity. There are also all the non-food organic and "green" and alternative items to include, such as cleaning products, soaps, shampoos, incense and aromatherapy oils.

Paving and decking

Decking is particularly in fashion now, and people will always want good old-fashioned patios or slabs somewhere in the garden. The secret of laying either of these successfully is preparing the ground properly, so everything stays level. Decking is often set on polythene, with holes cut for plants and drainage. There are numerous methods for slabs; if going onto soil dig down and lay a hard-core of rubble for drainage, then top it with sand and tamp this well down. The sand allows you to manoeuvre the slabs into exact position by tapping and sliding them. Afterwards brush more sand over to bind the whole surface tight. Do remember paving slabs are *heavy* and it's easy to hurt your back. Watching a group of navvies working on a street pavement for a day is by far the best education, followed by a trial run in your own garden before you attempt your first professional job. If you have basic bricklaying skills you could build permanent barbecue areas. See Gardening.

Personalised clocks

This is another great hobby business for those that like fiddling around with small parts and creating something original. A variety of basic clock mechanisms are available by mail order. All you have to do is mount them into a surround, which celebrates the name and/or lifestyle of the recipient. For a football fan for example, paint the mounting green with white goal posts and pitch markings. Or take photographs of relevant scenes, copy and mount them behind Perspex around the clock dial. Build up a range of common interest clocks – golf, football, sailing, motoring etc. and sell at Craft Fairs and to shops. You can also insert the person's name. Take special requests and charge a bit more. Have a good time…!

Personal shopper

This can either involve getting the groceries in for busy working people, or taking them round interior design stores picking out tiles, paints, wallpaper and furnishings.

If you've a flair for the latter it can be a very congenial job. Get to know the bespoke stores at the higher end of the market, and keep up with new products and ranges.

People are prepared to spend enormous amounts on their homes, but are desperate for a shrewd helping hand to plan and purchase what they want. Often, they don't even know what they want, and will willingly pay you an hourly rate for taking them out and talking over the options. So if you enjoy helping other people spend their money, get your Personal Shopper business cards printed now. See Interior Design.

Personal trainer

If you're a fitness freak or have been an athlete yourself, why not pass on your training tips to others. Nearly everyone is health conscious these days, but sedentary workers in particular need a bit of motivation. Always recommend people to check with their doctor before they begin any routines with you. Your work might be as simple as going out jogging with a client, to writing them a full weekly exercise and diet programme and making sure they stick to it. Read about sports psychology and learn about concentration and the all-important "pain barrier". Now get those knees up...one two, one two!

Pet supplies

People spend a fortune on their pets, especially if they buy the best nutritionally balanced foods. These come in large bulky packs and are a bit of a chore to pick up from the shops. You can start out by buying the food retail and simply delivering it, together with other pet-related items, to your customers. As soon as possible, source your products at wholesale prices. You'll need a garage or other space to store it, but being mostly dried the high-nutrition brands have a long shelf life and don't require refrigeration. See Dog Walking/Grooming and Cattery.

Picture framing

True, you can buy all sorts of ready-made picture frames these days. What you don't so often find is something unique, provided with care and attention. What do people want framed? All the cherished events of life; photos of their engagement, wedding, and honeymoon, pictures of their children from the time they are born, grow, graduate from university, get married, have children...you get the picture! Then there's certificates, awards, photos of meeting Mickey Mouse in Disneyland, shaking hands with Prince Charles or David Beckham – memorable pictures deserve a superior frame. Specialist shops can supply all your mouldings, samples of which you can take for clients to choose. Make or buy a mitre block to cut the 45 degree angles on the moulding. You'll also need a small saw, proper card for the mountings and backing and craft knives to cut it. Plus a glasscutter, panel pins and tape. You can include eyes and cord for hanging, and don't forget to stick your contact label on the back.

Photographer

David Bailey – who's he? If you don't remember the advert he was a top fashion and celebrity snapper. The art of photography is not vast technical expertise, but having an "eye" for a great picture, and a bit of charisma to boot. Mainstream demand will be for weddings and related family events, where you'll often need crowd management skills too! Actors and entertainers need to update their publicity shots regularly and this can be a good source of income on weekdays. Either do the shoot at their place or in your living room. Rig up a suitable backdrop and a couple of strong lights. If you don't already have it, second-hand gear can be perfectly serviceable. See Freelance Press Photographer.

Removals

If you're reasonably fit and strong, this is a solid, traditional business you can always make money from. If you prefer to leave the heavy lifting to others, then bring your sons or some young lads on board and teach them how to handle everything from grand pianos to aspidistras with the same skill and care. Logistics is a key factor in removals, and if you can pick up a load close to where you drop one off, it's clearly advantageous. If you're just a "man and a van" stick a card in your local newsagents for a month or so and work will come before long. Drop leaflets at houses with "For Sale" signs up and leave your card with estate agents too. As always, stress the personal service aspect of what you provide.

Rent a room

If you have a spare room at home it is a potential source of income for virtually no effort. Most of what you earn will probably not be liable for tax. Do consider the implications first. Unless you have a separate entrance to the proposed room, your lodger will use your front door, hall and stairs - and what about the bathroom and kitchen? Maybe you live alone and will be glad of a little company around the house as well as extra money. Try if possible to find someone who'll not only pay you the rent on time, but will be easy to get on with. Without being too heavy, lay down some basic ground rules before any agreements are made and this should avoid problems.

There are agencies which offer temporary accommodation to overseas students and this might be a good bet if you prefer a regular turnover of paying guests. If you supply breakfast and/or dinner it will boost your income. See Tour Guide.

Re-pointing

Older properties' brickwork suffers from crumbling mortar as the years go by. It is essential that this is restored to ensure the long-term stability of the house. Re-pointing involves raking out the loose mortar to a depth of a centimetre or two and refilling with correctly mixed fresh mortar. Consult a DIY or building manual for the precise techniques, as it's important to get things like the mortar mix and finish correct, to ensure a sound job. Leaflet houses that are clearly in need of re-pointing.

For larger properties i.e. over two floors high, you'll need scaffolding, but you should be able to get plenty of work from the average two-up two-down, where a secured ladder moved at intervals round the property should provide adequate access.

Room divider screens

In modern open-plan houses the very spaciousness of the room design can, on occasion, be a problem in disguise. Dad wants to watch Coronation Street while the kids do their homework on the table, or Mum's on the phone to her sister in Australia while Uncle Kevin's telling a long, complicated joke over a glass of home-brew - a recipe for chaos and frayed tempers. A traditional, three-piece screen can solve this problem. It won't cut out noise, but it will give that sense of privacy and two separate areas, allowing families to enjoy different activities in close proximity. All you need are three pieces of plywood about six-foot tall and hinges to join them. Use mouldings and fancy trim for the edges and varnish or paint. You could also make some arty Victorian style screens by pasting old pictures and cuttings, pieces of wallpaper etc. onto the surface and clear varnishing over them. When not required the screen can be folded flat and stored under the stairs or elsewhere out of sight. Make chi-chi bedroom versions and kids' themed screens, which they can put their own designs on. See Shelving.

Rubbish clearance

Getting rid of unwanted items is a major problem. In both urban and rural areas, what do you do with an old TV, washing machine, sacks of rubble, broken bicycle, old tyres and all manner of other unwanted rubbish? Quite rightly, there are strict penalties for fly-tipping. People have the choice of renting a skip, which can be costly and too large for the amount of rubbish they have, or loading up their car and taking a long drive to the nearest corporation dump. Relieve them of this burden - and a modest amount of their cash – by bagging up and neatly removing their unsightly and unwanted mounds of junk for them. You may often be able to salvage, repair and sell certain items – old pieces of furniture for example – rather than take them to the dump, thereby doing your bit for the environment and earning yourself a bonus. Where there's muck there's brass!

Sandwich delivery

Make your rounds of sandwiches at home in a clean kitchen early morning and then make your rounds of the workplaces from about 10am onwards. Offices often have sandwich bars close by, but staff may appreciate your personal desk-side delivery when they're too busy to pop out. Industrial estates are a good bet as they're often in the middle of nowhere. Get to know your regulars and they'll stay loyal. Encourage special requests and provide a few novel fillings – honey and peanut butter is surprisingly popular! Offer to cater for staff parties, conferences etc. too.   See Catering.

Sash window repairs

There aren't many traditional apprentice-trained carpenters about nowadays, and these are the guys who understood the hidden mysteries of the box-sash - a beautifully simple and elegant mechanism for opening and closing the classic sash window with ease. What usually needs fixing is the sash-cord, which wears and breaks over time, leaving the window with no visible or in this case invisible means of support. For it is the unseen sash-weights, enclosed in the vertical box-frame either side of the window, which drops when the cords snap. First make sure the sure the upper window is safely braced up with batons – if not it could drop down and smash the glass. To gain access to the box, gently prise off the thin beading and open the side-facing wooden panel. You will find the fallen sash-weight standing at the bottom. Remove the broken cord and feed a new one over the pulley at the top and attach the ends to the window and the weight. Test for the correct length by opening and closing. Close up the wooden box frame and replace the beading, pinning and touching up the paintwork if necessary. This is the perfect business to compliment Window Cleaning.

Second-hand furniture

If you've got a van you can start this business straight away. There's no stigma on second-hand furniture nowadays and many people positively prefer it as being better made and having more character. Popular items are your basic wooden dining sets especially the old hoop-back chairs and draw-leaf tables. Buy your stock at auctions and offer house-clearance services. Trendy shabby-chic restaurants now like old odd bits and pieces of wooden furniture, so be on the lookout for any premises undergoing conversion and drop your card in.

Self-defence classes

Hire a room in a leisure centre for groups, but you can also offer this kind of tuition one-to-one. If you have formal qualifications put these on your posters/flyers. If your training comes via another profession such as security work, police or the services, always stress your credentials, as it will impart confidence. There are certain considerations to working with children, such as having undergone CRB and other checks. If can fulfil these criteria, then signing up juniors can make for a very successful business; parents are often keen for their children – girls and boys – to learn a martial art. The benefits in terms of mental and physical discipline, confidence and fitness are well known. See also Personal Trainer and Life Coach.

Shelving

In modern dwellings, space is very much at a premium. Space for books, CDs, DVDs, files and all the other stuff people accumulate, especially as families expand. The expense of moving or building an extension can be forestalled by simply putting up a few shelves. Even if they have the skills, actually getting round to doing it however is one job too many for a lot of people. Ready-made shelf units rarely fit the dimensions and contours of the homeowner's own walls, and this is where tailor-made shelving is the ideal solution to their problems. The cheapest and strongest material is plywood with thick wooden uprights and say, 2x1 batten supports on the walls. When painted, such constructions can look very classy indeed. Drop your leaflets into those period terraced houses; they all have chimney alcoves which are just crying out for some nice looking shelving. Take a colour picture of your first completed job and print onto your leaflet.

Shoe shine boy

Or girl! Print some leaflets and take around big offices. Arrange to come in say once a day and work your way around the desks for whoever wants a brilliantly polished pair of shoes, gleaming and ready for that top-notch lunch or dinner engagement. The great thing is the client doesn't even have to come off the phone. They can carry on selling stocks, bonds, insurance or whatever while you merrily buff away, then toss you a couple of quid or whatever fee you decide on. All you essentially need is black, brown and neutral polishes, brushes and dusters, and small footrest. Make your image more classy/fun with a cap and tunic or t-shirt with your logo on.

Soft toys

If you've a sewing machine and a soft spot for cuddly teddies, get cracking making your own unique range of bears, rag dolls, lions, tigers, pandas and every other type of animal that children love. Get all your child-safe stuffing material and eyes from craft suppliers. You could also make glove puppets, school bags and pyjama cases with character faces on. Approach playgroups and nurseries with some samples and, if your products are pleasing, reasonably priced and that little bit different, you'll be sure to get orders.

Speech writing

A Best Man will often agonise over his speech, as will the Bride's father, or anyone else who has to deliver some hopefully well-chosen words at a special occasion. You don't have to be good speaker yourself to write excellent speeches for other people, you just need to be aware of etiquette, have a sense of humour and be prepared to adapt a general formula to different people. The trick is to sprinkle the jokes liberally, but avoid trying to be clever or aiming to impress with obscure quotations or high-minded references. A good speech is not an opportunity for the speaker to show off, but to make his or her audience feel good. See Wedding Planner, Photographer, Caterer, Cake Decorating.

Sports coach

Whatever your sport, they'll be people who'd like to learn it or improve. Solo games are ideal, and tennis is a particular favourite, especially when the summer months arrive. Golf is now attracting a larger take-up, with many more women keen to learn. Leave your card at relevant clubs and leisure centres and quote an hourly rate, with discount for pairs and small groups. A good combination of coaching services is an outdoor game for the warmer seasons and one you can switch to in autumn and winter, such as squash or badminton. See Personal Trainer

Swimming instructor

Not everyone has learnt to swim by adulthood. It's often a source of great regret, especially at holiday time when others are splashing joyfully in the sea. They'd love to learn now, but understandably don't want to suffer the sort sergeant-major type with clipboard and whistle so often found leading swimming classes. So, if you can swim yourself and have a sympathetic manner, there's no reason why you can't earn good money teaching others this valuable and enjoyable skill.

You will need, obviously, water. A local authority pool is best, with lifeguards on hand. For one-to-one tuition you can probably just take your pupil along, but for a group you'll probably need to book your own session. It'll help to get an official qualification, and the Amateur Swimming Association run instructor courses. You should also consider getting a life-saving certificate and a relevant insurance policy.

Think about running "learn to swim" holidays either in the UK or abroad; everyone will have a great time and hopefully, by the end they are all swimming for the first time.

Tiling

Have you seen the number of tile shops about these days? The nation it seems has gone "tile crazy" and the trend looks set to continue. Tiling is not particularly difficult to learn but does require a little thought and care. Plastic spacers, special adhesives and glues make things easier, and if you're doing large jobs, a heavy-duty tile cutter is a sound investment. The tile shops will usually offer plenty of advice. One new development is the growing popularity of "wet rooms". These are bathrooms or shower areas where the whole room is tiled over, floor to ceiling, allowing the user to splash about with abandon and let the water go anywhere, till it all runs off to a central drain. If you do get asked to create a wet room, ask the client to make sure their floor can take the weight of the tiles, especially if they're thinking about marble or stone slabs. Don't forget to show your trade card and request a discount whenever you buy your tiles.

Tour guide

If you live in a place of great historical interest, it no doubt attracts lots of visitors. There are also probably a lot of official tours on offer. If so, offer something that's a bit different. Take couples in your own car and beat the coach jams around the museums. Show them the best places to get lunch, drinks and dinner, avoiding the usual rip-off merchants. Research the monuments and history so you can give a really in-depth commentary as good as the big tour operators and books. Introduce them to local flea markets, interesting pubs and the lifestyle of people who actually live in the area. Walking tours are a good idea if you and your clients are fit enough to be car-free and carefree. And if you think there's nothing to attract visitors to your home area, examine it more closely. Are there famous ex-residents - composers, authors, statesmen or pop stars? If so you can bet they have a fan club or society somewhere in the world. Study your local Blue Plaques and check the web. Contact any relevant groups and offer your personal guided tour of the area. In Bromley for example were born both H.G. Wells and David Bowie. It's not only the past people want to come and see; if you live in an area of exciting change, artistic endeavour or great natural beauty - Docklands, the Eden Project or Dartmoor for example – then you have a magnet at your disposal. Activate it by writing to relevant groups worldwide – retirement and cultural societies etc and offer a general hosting service – arranging accommodation, meeting, greeting and showing them a good time.

Tree surgery

To start by stating the obvious, you'll need a head for heights. You'll also need public liability insurance before you start actually climbing. You can however obtain your first job on a shoestring budget. A chain saw isn't essential, unless you're tackling very large jobs. Many householders will appreciate someone working quietly with a handsaw and loppers. Make sure you establish exactly how much branch and foliage requires removal before and as you proceed. You can begin by operating this business as an extension of Gardening, and to obtain more specialist status contact the Arboricultural Association.

Upholstery

What we're really talking about here is re-upholstery. Repairing period armchairs, settees and chaise lounges whose seats and backs have collapsed. There is a special tool for this work called a 'stretcher' for drawing the webbing across the wooden frame of the seat and holding it taut while you pin everything in place. There are various materials you can use for the "stuffing", including kapok and traditional horsehair. If you do use foam check it's the flameproof type. You may also find it useful to learn leatherwork. Prime customers are likely to be the elderly and people in Victorian and Edwardian properties, who generally have period furniture too. You can either offer to collect and return items, or carry out the work in the customer's own home. As with all types of restoration, it is pleasing to be able to breathe new life into beautiful old things. And there's always the remote chance of finding a wad of banknotes stuffed down the back of a sofa.

Vintage record dealing

Ever been at a boot sale or in an Oxfam shop and seen a punter who's got his head stuck into a box of old records with the intensity of a ferret down a rabbit hole? If so you'll have witnessed a "vinyl trader" at work. These guys are on the lookout for rare grooves, anything they can pick up for a pound and sell to fanatical collectors for a seriously big profit. Elvis, the Sex Pistols, Beatles, Oasis, even Abba – there's someone, somewhere, interested in almost every band that's ever been. By far the best way to deal in vintage vinyl is via the Internet, enabling you to reach thousands of collectors worldwide.

Virtual PA

A lot of entrepreneurs and small businesses have administration needs but not sufficient to directly employ a secretary. With a virtual PA they can get reports, surveys, letters, quotes and whatever else typed up as and when required and receive a simple invoice at the end of the month. You can also offer telephone answering, either full-time or diverted to you when your client is too busy to take calls. Obviously you'll earn more with multiple clients, so in the interests of their image, get some telephone technology that'll route different numbers into your line and tell you which number's being called. You can then answer in the appropriate company name. The appeal of a virtual PA is flexibility – your clients only pay for what they ask you to do. Charge a realistic rate per thousand words for typing and a nominal amount for each call you receive on their behalf.

Walking tours

These can last for one or two hours during the evening or day, weekends or weekdays, and cover a particular route in your local area. What you need to find is a theme. The Jack the Ripper tour of White chapel has been popular for many years. Is there potential for something similar near to you? If not, think something up – a local legend or ghost story, a historical event around which you can spin a yarn. A pub-crawl is elevated to a "cultural evening" by a little learning and speculation! Charge a modest fee per person and if possible sell any relevant souvenirs to your punters.

Washing machine installation

If you've plumbed in your own washing machine you can do the same for others and earn money from it. All the hoses and clips can be picked up at the DIY store, if they're not supplied with the machine. Sometimes people want their machine moved, from a kitchen into a utility room extension or when they move house. Apart from shifting the weight of the machine, simple plumbing operations are a nightmare for some folk. Dishwashers are becoming more popular now, and you can provide the same service for these. Learn about the workings and common problems of domestic appliances and you'll soon be offering basic repairs and maintenance too.

Wedding planner

Organising a wedding can be very stressful – especially if it's your own! There are lots of elements that need to be co-ordinated, and if you thrive on adrenalin then you'll be in your element as a wedding planner. People tend to book a year or more in advance in order to secure a venue. Get to know a range of suitable places, not only in your own area – people often want somewhere miles from where they now live. Make contact with caterers, photographers, car hire firms, DJs, bands and vicars! Be prepared to deal with "people problems" especially over seating plans and future in-laws. Be calm, orderly and get all your estimates – including your own charges – agreed well in advance of the event. You'll also be a shoulder to cry on at times, so keep a box of tissues, tea and sympathy at the ready.

Window cleaning

Do you have fond memories of "Confessions of a Window Cleaner"? Well it's not all soapsuds and bored housewives. However, people do welcome a window cleaner with open arms these days, certainly those of the domestic variety, as they're a rare breed. If you have a ladder and a van, your only other real investment is one of those squeegee wipers and a couple of lengths of scrim, which is a special non-smearing cloth available from cleaning suppliers. You will also need some customers. Drop fifty of so leaflets through doors and your phone will soon be ringing. Prime time to start is when the clocks change in the spring, when people returning home from work suddenly see their filthy panes for the first time in months.

Wooden toys

There is just something nice about wood. Unlike most plastic toys, wood feels "real" and pleasant to handle, especially when it's crafted into chunky pull-along trains and trucks for young hands to enjoy. The shapes you'll need are all basic and you can buy ready-turned wheels and dowelling for axles from hobby suppliers. Smooth all surfaces to eradicate any chance of splinters and if using any kind of paint, check health and safety regulations. As soon as you have a basic range, take some items round the more arty children's wear and toyshops. Try to sell straight on if possible, otherwise offer on sale or return. To cut out the middleman, consider a website and/or mail order advertising. See Craft Fairs and Dolls Houses.

The biggest idea of all

The greatest idea of all is to get stimulated with the material in these four chapters. Add this together with your own aptitudes, skills, interests and passions and come up with your own unique services or product that you can start marketing cost effectively!

What to do next

If you have enjoyed these pages, we have already 'met.' Let's 'meet' again by going to www.ukbizguru.com or www.Wealth.co.uk.

CHAPTER FOUR

COMPOUND GROWTH

I don't have too many regrets in my live, but if I do have one, it was not being able to meet the late great Joe Karbo, the author of the renowned *'Lazy Mans Way to Riches'* when I was invited out to Huntington Beach in California in 1979. Joe's favourite saying was that 'Most people are too busy earning a living to make any real money' and this chapter is all about alerting you to constantly working with principles that will make you rich.

Unfortunately Joe was too ill to keep his appointment with me, but I spent a highly entertaining and informative day with his stepson, Jay Flanagan, which was the next best thing. During the day Jay shared many secrets with me and also shared the most exciting day of his life when $480,000 came tumbling through his mailbox in small cheques. At that juncture he knew Karbo, as he was affectionately called, really had taught him the secrets of copy writing and mail order promotion. As well as giving me a guided tour of the most famous mail order company in the world, and sharing its philosophy, Jay was kind enough to take me to lunch at the *Queen Mary* which was then a floating restaurant berthed nearby at Long Beach, where we had a delicious Lobster Thermidor lunch and a selection of Californian wines. I shall never forget the glimpse of hedonistic pleasure; the glamorous grand interiors in art deco, the vast 700-seater dining room with high ceilings with a centrepiece of a giant map of the North Atlantic, individual tables were laid with best silver and cut glass, in the centre a vase of red roses. This queen dazzled her guests with her rich woods, gold, glass and massive uplights, chandeliers, ornate staircases, massive sculptured brass doors, and everywhere huge arrays of beautifully arranged flowers. In this opulent setting we discussed Karbo's method of compounding simple ideas into massive growth. On the return trip to Huntington, and as an extra special treat, because it was my first time in the States, we did a quick detour to see Howard Hughes *Spruce Goose* in the largest geodesic dome in the world. Which, as an aside, leads me to another tip I learned from the 'families'. This is that on ones travels, try to drop off at places of interest; museums, beauty spots, landmarks, because you never know when you'll pass that way again, if ever. Enjoy the journey, not just the destination. This proved to be the case here. I have never been back to Long Beach and I'm glad we took advantage of the moment.

But I digress, back to Karbo's formula for compound growth. Taking Joes' example of investing $1000, you can become a millionaire in the mail order business in forty weeks just by compounding at 20%. Which is quite possible if you have a good product, good copy, a hard hitting headline and the Gods are with you. Karbo's formula is to start with small test adverts and then re-investing the capital and profits, start snowballing up your advertising campaign, until you are running full page adverts in the national press. I can certainly remember a time when Karbo was advertising 'Lazy' simultaneously in the *Los Angeles Times, New York Times*, and the *Chicago Tribune* as well as hundreds of business and general interest magazines. Karbo proved his 40 weeks to millionaire status with 20% compound growth, many times personally, but what is even more exciting, is that over the years hundreds of his readers have accomplished similar results.

On a footnote, I have to say that this was no Lazy Way to Riches. Karbo's set up was like a massive aircraft hangar that was racked out from head to toe in shelving and carried thousands of mail order products, not just his famous books. There were three or four jitter-bugs scurrying around at a rate of knots, ferrying books, vitamins and other mail order products to various parts of the warehouse, and at least 40 staff all busy making computer entries, stuffing packages and answering phones. As I left I logged the thought that this was a hive of industry, and if one is to make a fortune you have got to get into a real serious business, turning over real products and making real money. It was an eye-opener to say the very least, and I'm glad I had this particular wake-up-call early on in my entrepreneurial career.

Weekly wages and monthly salaries

The majority of people have an inbuilt programme that usually revolves around either a weekly wage or a monthly salary. Nothing wrong with that, so long as we learn to free the shackles and increase the shekels, by doing something on our own account.

This philosophy is all about doing things differently, seeing things from another angle, and trying to work with proven success techniques that can yield very big dividends. The majority of 'get rich' contenders do not have those techniques as part of their everyday vocabulary, but the methodologies are very much the vocabulary of the 'families'.

Even when the people who are not in the inner circle do get a little glimmer of hope they tend to dabble in the theories and the motivational seminar stories that leave one glowing and hoping. Stories such as the one where the pauper agrees to take from the King a grain of rice for his wares, across a chess set, on the understanding that each day the grains of rice double from the previous day. Little does the King realise, by the time he has reached the last square, the number of grains equals more rice than there is in the whole wide world. Another knave becomes a millionaire by agreeing to take a pound for his labour, doubling up every day for 32 days, and he too becomes a millionaire.

What about in actual practice

For the past thirty years I have made myself busy getting my mind around, and witnessing what the 'families' do in real life to snowball their means up to gigantic proportions and how they repeatedly turn these examples of massive growth and abundance into reality. I have made enormous strides forward for myself in everyday things, aligning myself with age old principles that work in creating massive dividends and trying hard to get away from a heavily programmed culture and mindset of working for a living, wages and salaries. I have had to work hard at it, because it was initially a very alien philosophy to me.

Compound interest

Often referred to as the eighth wonder of the world, compound interest is one of the amazing ways in which money can grow. Banks make billions of pounds profit every year and they do so by using the law of compound interest. The most common everyday example that most people come into contact with, is on their own mortgages. When you consider that most people pay on average three times what they actually borrowed for their houses in the first place you can see the power of compound interest. What you must make every endeavour to do is get on the receiving end of the principle, i.e. receive compound interest on your savings and your investments. There are many absolutely free completely downloadable Compound Interest Calculators on the Internet and you could do no better than to download one onto your computer and spend a few hours at your leisure, educating yourself, family and your team about compound interest.

Equity release - scheme or scam

Over the recent years there has been an escalation of people releasing the equity in their homes. Nothing wrong with that per se, people taking advantage of the huge increase in property prices has allowed many pensioners and indeed others to find themselves with massive amounts of equity in their homes.

What is wrong is the people don't investigate and see what options are available to them and this results in them taking the first cash offer that is made to them which results, more often than not, in having to pay exorbitant rates of interest, for what amounts to a simple mortgage or re-mortgage. Only when the incumbent has difficulty keeping up the new repayments does someone point out the error of their ways and that they could have released the equity much more cost effectively, had it only been done another way.

This brings me back to education with particular emphasis on numeracy. The 'families' are well informed and well educated and know intuitively how to calculate interest rates, where to buy the cheapest money, after all it is only a commodity, and exactly where to dig out and explore for options. People outside the 'inner circle' are often confused, lazy, intimidated, uninformed, uneducated and know little about the secrets of money.

Percentage game

I have told the story before, but it's an old favourite of mine. There was a scrap metal dealer who was a billionaire, who was being interviewed for a TV show. The researcher had done his homework and quizzed; 'You've made it no secret, you are illiterate and innumerate, but you're a billionaire. What's the secret of your fabulous success?' 'Well' replied the scrap dealer, puffing on a Corona, 'It's easy! I buy scrap metal for £100 a ton and sell it for £300 a ton. There's 2% for a start!'

I have learned, over the years, that sometimes it serves little purpose to talk about the massive percentages that can be attained in business by those in the know, that sometimes those percentages as so far removed from normal everyday reality, you tend to lose all credibility when you talk them. Further, research that I have done over a ten year period shows that over 38% of the people in business on their own account are innumerate, and the situation is getting worse, daily.

I have already mentioned that over the years I have deliberately tried to align myself with methodologies that create massive returns. Let me give you an example. I worked within a particular network marketing company to help restructure their presentation that they thought was not working as efficiently as it could, because the company was now quite mature. The guy who was making the presentation had a 'Diamond' in his up-line that was earning $1,000,000 a month on a regular basis and he made a point of announcing that fact at every possible opportunity. He had the effect of turning people off, because although it was true, most people who heard the pitch could not equate to those fabulous incomes. What we did was completely rework the presentation, never once mentioning the obscene incomes people were making, but talked about an opportunity to earn an extra $200 or $300 a month, with much more money available, for ambitious people who really wanted to go for it. This trick worked magically and the exponential growth the company had experienced previously was now back on line. People could relate to earning an extra $100 or $300 a month, but when $1,000,000 a month was mentioned, schizoma took over and people eyes glazed over.

Now that I have laid out my stall, I will say that most people can get their minds around a Building Society paying an interest rate of 6% per annum because they have seen this quoted many times, read about similar figures in the press or seen it on the TV and chances are they may even have money of their own in a building society. They have many reference points. Yes, 6% sounds about right!

The 'families' teach, train and educate from a very early age to think in terms of much higher rates of interest and growth that can be made on a regular basis. A built-in acceptance of massive returns. It becomes part of their vocabulary, belief system and everyday life.

Without getting into detail about how to buy unquoted securities, for the time being, what I will say is that by trading in the Shares of start-up companies and early stage companies 3000% to 6000% growth is common place, and you can do it relatively risk free if you follow certain strategies.

There is magic in penny shares, which is the pinnacle of this philosophy. If you buy Shares at 5p and sell them for 55p you already have 1000% profit. If you buy Shares at 5p and then sell at £1.05p you have 2000%, and if you buy at 5p and sell at £1.55p you have 3000%. I have mentioned my partner Bruce on a number of occasions, and his shares in Applied Holographics PLC shot from 5p to £6.80 and that's a whopping 13,500% profit. No wonder Bruce drinks champagne by the Jeroboam! As they say in the City, 'Jolly heady stuff. What?'

For those readers that are not particularly numerate with percentages, perhaps what you need you to do is access the Internet or go to the local bookstore and get some information on maths and percentages and familiarise yourself with growths at this unusually high level. For now, accept what I am telling you, buying and selling shares at these prices really happens, for those in the know, on a regular basis.

Compound interest

My introduction to compound interest was when I decided to track back a £100 investment I had made in my motorcycle shop. This was just one of the £100 that I followed through for a year and it went, albeit approximately, like this:

Starting at the beginning of the investment cycle one hot Saturday afternoon in June I purchased a Triumph Tiger Cub Scrambler for £100. That same day I sold the motorcycle for £120 in cash and also took in part exchange a Go-Kart and three BSA engines, a couple of Norton wheels and a big box of assorted motorcycle junk. I remember it well because my mechanic said to me 'You must be mad. If only you had waited a week or two, you could have got two hundred pounds for it, maybe more!'

Now this guy was a good mechanic, but he didn't know what I know. That is to take a profit and in particular to take a part exchange at the same time. That is how compound growth is really created. And

156

don't forget I didn't wait 365 days for my £20 cash profit; I got that within hours of outlaying the money and still had a Go-Kart and piles of other beautiful spares to sell as well. It is an important point to note, when I bought stuff it was junk, and when I sold it was hard to get hold of spares, collector's items, vintage parts and above everything 'It's just what you need, Sir.'

To take the £100 investment story through to a 365 day conclusion will drive you to distraction and also take up three reams of A4 paper. Suffice to say I now re-invested the £100 plus the £20 profit into more second-hand motorcycles and parts. Plus I sold the three engines and wheels and all the beautiful spares in the box of junk. I took cash on some deals but mostly I encouraged cash and part exchange of more junk that turned into beautiful spares, the moment the seller walked out the door. It really is amazing to think when people are done with something in their lives it becomes junk, and when people desperately need that same part, it is a vintage spare, a collector's item.

The real power of compound growth is that you get compounding on the compounding on the compounding! It's as though each deal splits off and has children of its own, who have children, who in turn have more children and those children have even more children. When an atom is split, the massive power released is not as a result of splitting a single atom. The power is released as a result of the chain reaction it causes, which splits more atoms that split even more atoms, exponentially. Now that's powerful!

By the end of the year the original investment had split into literally hundreds of wheels, engines, bikes, parts that all lead into further deals that split off into further deals and the £100 grew exponentially and compounded all the way to the bank. On the strength of it I opened seven motorcycle shops and two second-hand furniture shops that operated on the same principle. In actual fact I even had a big sign in my Wimbledon shop stating 'We Buy Junk and Sell Antiques.' It was a lot of fun and I learned about compound growth on a daily basis and laughed all the way to the bank!

In the mid-seventies, when I had my shops, you could earn maybe 6% at a Building Society on your money. In simple terms if you invested a £100, quite a lot of money in the early seventies, when most skilled tradesmen earned just over £30 a week, at the end of the year it would be worth £106. This much I understood. So real the real lesson I learned was never to invest £100 for 6% interest when 1000's of per cent was available, for the taking, if you invested it in your own business, and generated compound growth!

I got my hands dirty

Time over I see eager seminar participants, many of them seminar junkies, desperately seeking success, just looking for that one gem that is going to turn their lives around. In a nutshell, what I see is thousands of people who want success, but very few who want to get their hands dirty, even fewer willing to take a risk and fewer still willing take on board that you have to make a start, even when circumstances aren't perfect, perhaps have a few failures, maybe even a thousand failures like Edison, before you reach the land of Milk and Honey or get your electric light bulb invention to work.

I see a disturbing trend, that I am in the process of reversing, toward people's focus being on NLP, meditation, visualisation, spirituality, nothing wrong with all these since I introduced them to the business and sales arena in 1981 in 'Talk and Grow Rich'. I feel what is needed now is a much more pragmatic success philosophy which allows people to use all that good stuff, but at the same time realising that to create financial freedom and abundance you have got to get in the stream of business, selling products or services.

The lily pond

Bruce Snyder, my partner of nearly twenty years, a scientist, physicist and mathematician, once showed me columns and columns of figures neatly illustrating how companies very quickly expand from a few million pounds of turnover to a few billion in turnover and it's been done many times, particularly with companies who use quoted paper to pay for the acquisitions.

Not being particularly numerate, I wrestled with these figures for weeks, because I knew there was magic in them, and then it hit me. I had a Eureka! I grabbed a sheet of paper and drew out a lily pond that showed quite literally how a company doing £10m acquires another company doing the same, another £10m. Then the enlarged £20m company acquires another company whose turnover is in the region of £20m. Then that £40m turnover group acquires another company turning over £40m.

The enlarged £80m group, yes you guessed it, acquires another £80m turnover company, then the £160m group acquires another company turning over £160m making a combined group turnover of £320m. The £320m company acquires another £320m company then the £640m turnover group acquires one the same or similar size making a group business of over billion pounds turnover. Using this methodology with six acquisitions a company can go from £10m turnover to a billion pounds turnover, often very quickly.

There is so much scope for acquisitive vehicles I just cannot imagine why more companies don't go on the acquisition trail and go from zero to hero in less than five years. I can think of well over two dozen fragmented 'cottage industries' that would benefit tremendously from additional capital, professional management, combined buying power and are screaming out to be pulled together by an acquisitive team.

I have analysed many acquisitive vehicles including Blue Arrow, Pollypeck, Virgin, and many others and the Chairmen of these groups used exactly this methodology described here. It is not a theory.

As an addendum to my story, the very same evening I drew out my lily pond, I was strolling through St James's Park idling the time away, eating ice cream and watching Canadian Geese and swans, waiting for my beautiful young lady Elisabeth, now my wife, to turn up with a lovely picnic in a wicker hamper. The picnic was to consist of lobster tails, tiger prawns and salmon as well as some Russian caviar with fresh brown bread and lemon slices. I didn't know what the main course was going to be, that was going to be a surprise! As I was sitting on the bench I was earwigging on another couples conversation. What caught me was the guy's accent, and because I love phonetics, I was trying to work out whether the gentleman was from Leeds or Doncaster, but couldn't quite place it. He said to his wife in thick Yorkshire dialect "Eh by gum petal, it's a lovely pond that, but I'll tell you where they went wrong. You see the "ejuts" have planted water lilies in one corner of the pond. What they don't realise is those plants double in size every year and in five years the whole pond will be covered in lilies." I love 'an omen.' I thought 'Gotcha!'

You're always working on big deals

One of my protégés, Peter Segal often pops into my office to discuss various clients of his or to see what I'm up to. He mentioned to me recently, 'It's a funny thing you know. Every time I come here you're always working on big deals, either your own or someone else's.' He continued 'That tells me something. I'm spending far too much of my time keeping my head above water and dealing with small clients. I'm concentrating hard on making a living and you're concentrating hard on making a fortune.' Now there's a gem for you!

Networking and MLM

My books have now been in the global market place since 1975. Over that period of time I can honestly say that I have worked with just about every major Network Marketing Company in the world and hundreds of the smaller ones, in one capacity or another, be it training, sales or marketing within the field organisation or advising at corporate level in the companies.

I have worked with over 280 'Diamonds', many of whom are millionaires. I can tell you one thing that they have in common, and if there ever was a secret as to why people succeed in networking this is it. They focus all their energy on sponsoring just one person...that's it! Simple as that! They also create buzz so people don't drop out quicker than others are coming in. They understand the meaning 'critical mass'. When they sponsor their first person into their own personal network, they have created an incredible 100% growth. At that point they don't expect too much profit, but they do understand the power of one, so they celebrate! As soon as there are two networkers you can see the exponential nature of networking begin to work. If two people sponsor one each, that makes a total of four. If four people sponsor one each, that makes a total eight networkers. These are networkers as opposed to <u>notworkers</u>! If eight excited and motivated people sponsor one each, that makes sixteen. Sixteen networkers that are wholly focused, manage to sponsor only one each, making a grand total in the network of thirty two people and if each one of those does his bit and brings in one each that'll create a sixty four person down-line. It really is true that you need to walk the living rooms of the world if you want to walk the beaches of the world and when sixty four get into enough peoples living rooms and add one additional person each that's one hundred and twenty six people in the network and that when you have reached a critical mass and the money will come flooding in. Now that's truly powerful, and that's what networking is all about!

'What if?' is part of my vocabulary

I have noted that the 'families' always have a sharp pencil handy at all times and constantly jot down figures and notes on scraps of paper, whenever they have a spare moment, in a park, on a train, bus, or waiting for an appointment. Those figures may read; if I sold x number of books at 10% royalty I'd make £1,000, but perhaps if I published the book myself I'd made £200,000. On the other hand the notes may read, 'If I buy this house or this lot and split it up like so, I'll make so and so profit, perhaps there is another way of splitting it up. If I carried out additional work or used another architect, I could increase my returns threefold.'

Another favourite; 'If I invent a mail order product and I get 1% response rate of my mail shot I'll make x, I must find a way of increasing the price and getting 3% response, then I'll get y, which is a lot more! I must hone up my copy writing skills and if I only get a half per cent return, I must find a way of creating a very high-ticket value item.

People outside the circle just do not think like this on a day-to-day basis. For the 'families' making the figures work is an obsession! They are constantly playing with figures 'what if this' or 'what if that' and trying to create new angles where huge cash flows and profits can come from, hence deliberately putting themselves in the way of massive incomes streams. The other point that has just popped into my head is the 'families' have a very pragmatic way of viewing figures and they seem to know intuitively that 1% is a fantastic return and 3% is a dream. Other cultures gets carried away and immediately start talking about 10% or 20% returns, which are never going to happen.

Cash flow is king

Unbeknownst to ordinary mortals there are huge numbers of business owners who run massive cash - flow businesses with little or no profit, but make huge fortunes by investing their turnover on the overnight markets. Many businesses such as petrol stations, flight bucket shops, bookmakers use this method of creating wealth. It's a simple enough deal. You can make an arrangement with your bank to 'deposit overnight' funds that are in your account over a certain limit. These funds will be put on deposit, gaining interest on a special overnight deposit account. The interest rate may not be all that high, but it's money for old rope and, if your turnover is significant, it could mean massive additional profits for you.

Reality - what a concept!

One man's meat is another man's poison. Do you realise there are many things in life that affect the reality that we create for ourselves. What we ingest affects our perception and our reality. For arguments sake, if you were continually chewing on the cocoa leaf or marijuana plant, as is common in some cultures, that would definitely affect your perception and reality. Drinking lots of coffee or indulging in large amounts of alcohol will affect the reality you have created for yourself and you can ask any alcoholic who suffers from delirium tremens, where the waking and sleeping phases get out of sync through lack of sleep, what it's like to see a dream happening in front of your very eyes whilst wide-awake in broad daylight.

The reality in which you operate and the one you have created for yourself depends on hundreds of factors including; where you live, how you were educated, what you eat, drink and smoke, what religious beliefs you have been exposed to or not as the case may be. To create an alternative reality for yourself you have to do different things in your life and I'll share with you a few of the things I did to create a new reality in my own life, and I'm glad I did.

I stopped smoking a long time ago and for the last eight years I have been absolutely teetotal. I worked hard at cultivating millionaires and multi-millionaires as friends and went out of my way to make this happen. I made sure they were people who could teach me about compound interest and exponential growth. I make sure I read positive thinking books and tapes and also play other people's tapes to keep in me in positive reality. I also took time to make my own tapes that were personal to me. I made a point of teaching success and that has helped me more than anything. By teaching others I had to clear my own thinking and doing otherwise would have appeared to be very incongruent. I made sure I also ate at the best restaurants and drove the finest cars.

Viral marketing takes advantage of compounding

As one of the first entrepreneurs to introduce the City to the Internet, having spotted its massive potential in the States, I feel I have quite a lot to say and quite a lot to offer. When I first approached the City in 1994 my Xanadu PLC dream team consisted of two heavyweight telecoms guys who had taken companies into the billions and two other executives that had taken companies into the hundreds of millions. We pounded the doors of hundreds of City stockbrokers and VCs, wore out shoe leather and eventually made a number of very exciting presentations. I tried in layman terms to explain what the Internet was: that you stick a phone line in the back of the computer and network with other computers and send each other electronic mail and access all the information in the world. The most common response was 'Ron, we love you, love your team. But we don't even have computers in the office. What on earth are you talking about?' Now that was a hard sell and we did our presentation many times. However, I do give the stockbrokers their due. They listened intently, asked hundreds of questions and tried to get their minds around 'The story.' At the end of the day they just couldn't see it. However, we warmed the stockbrokers up for the next round of contenders and when they came around a few years later the stockbrokers were going, 'Wow, we've already heard about this, tell us more.' Sticking the telephone line into the back of the computer, sending e-mail and accessing massive amounts of information was now something they could get their minds around. I do know from my own experience that it is often the first entrepreneurs into a new marketplace that lose their shirts. They pay the price of education. Xanadu PLC was probably the first Dotcom fatality in the UK and was seen as a failure by many, but in reality it really was a huge success, not necessarily in financial terms but by helping open up a new market place where thousands of people are now going on to become millionaires.

I sincerely believe the Internet is still at the embryonic stage and all the growth is ahead of us. The massive restrictions in growth have nothing to do with limiting technology, but more to do with the telecom companies themselves who spend 10% of their time and resources on technology and 90% of their time and money trying to find out how to exploit it, and make money from it.

The Internet takes advantage of exponential growth and one of the first examples of that was Hotmail - a company that has its beginnings in HTML programming. Hot Mail used viral marketing techniques to get its subscribers and in its heyday was attracting some 126,000 new subscribers a week. Bill Gates saw the potential for the future and bought the company for some $300,000,000.

Viral marketing, compounding and exponential growth is so simple on the Internet. It consists of having a good website, message and product. Because of the ease of telling others about the wonderful product you have just seen, the viral nature takes off. Ten people tell ten people who tell ten people and suddenly the world knows. Already tens of billions of e-mails are being sent monthly and we haven't even started.

In the world of Grand Prix racing and F1 we all know and accept that 'Racing improves the breed'. What the majority of people don't realise is that hackers are doing the same thing for the Internet. Although I do not condone what they do, they are in effect the policemen of the Internet, forcing the telecoms, computer and software companies to make it a far better, faster, safer and more secure place to conduct business and pleasure.

Already the Internet has proved how it can shift billions of pounds worth of products, globally in a very short space of time. Gambling, sex and credit card transactions already run into billions. Once the telecoms companies work out how to exploit it for themselves they will supply conduits that can download films, seminars, music – in fact any information you want!

It may well be that the Internet will need massive external processing power to process the huge amounts of data that will become available on the Internet in the not too distant future. Huge, so far un-built computers like Ivor Catt's 'Kernal' that have 1000 times more capacity, processing power and speed than the largest mainframe Cray could process information outside the Internet and speed up massively.

I often smile to myself when using the Internet currently, it's often like watching paint dry and the concept of Bills Gates *Business @ The Speed of Thought* is amusing when the telecoms companies can keep you waiting in a queue for seemingly ages. But better things will come and those entrepreneurs and investors who are seeing the potential of compounding will be at the forefront of its massive growth.

Ted Nelson was one of the front-runners in the very early days of the Internet and he created the concept of the hyper-link. His Xanadu project was to establish a simple means of enabling every single bit of information in the world to be linked to every other bit of information. This is now finally happening on the Internet and eventually intelligent search engines will allow us to input massive amounts of information pertaining to the exact data we intend to retrieve and the search engines will bring back precise data based on the information and parameters we provided in the first place. Currently we can only type in a few words and it is still very much a hit or miss affair, but that won't always be the case. Ted Nelson never made any money in America during his Xanadu days but became best known for his eccentric habit of making hand held cine-camera movies about all his interviews and business meetings. Ted now spends most of his time in Japan where hopefully he is making oodles of money with his new partners.

Now, where am I leading with all this? Coming back to Karbo's compounding formula for making money in the mail order business and how Jay Flanagan received $480,000 through his letterbox in one day. A whole new world of even greater possibilities exist now for marketing products and services on the Internet and the products that are currently flying are products that actually show people how to market on the Internet. I estimate the sales of this type of e-book are already running into hundreds of millions of pounds.

1.   Get compound interest on your savings, investments and businesses.

2.   Understand compound interest racking up on your mortgage and do everything you can to reduce it.

3.   Think outside the box way beyond wages and salaries. Think of the big principles. Act on the big principles.

4.   You are much better off getting your hands dirty and be in with a chance of getting rich, rather than keeping them clean and having no chance at all.

5.   Get yourself a business where you can capitalise on compound growth.

6.   Use the lily pond effect to create exponential growth. Networks double in size quickly only when they have reached critical mass. Never forget the power of one.

7.   Play with figures and ideas continuously. Re-programme yourself to think of high growth and high returns.

8. If you work on small deals you may be lucky enough to keep your head above water. If you work on BIG deals, you may fail, but at least you are putting yourself in line to make a fortune. At the very least you will be putting yourself in the way of big money.

9. Potential is always about the future. Once you know what the growth is the potential has effectively gone.

BEST WISHES AND GOOD FORTUNE

RON G HOLLAND
Eureka Financial

Suite 8061
27 Old Gloucester Street
London
WC1N 3XX

www.RonHollandDirect.com
topbizguru@hotmail.com

Get free downloads and find out more about Ron G Holland's latest publications, mentoring and business ventures at:

www.wealth.co.uk